PRAISES & OFFENSES

PRAISES & OFFENSES:

THREE WOMEN POETS FROM THE DOMINICAN REPUBLIC

AÍDA CARTAGENA PORTALATÍN
ÁNGELA HERNÁNDEZ NÚÑEZ
YLONKA NACIDIT-PERDOMO

TRANSLATED FROM THE SPANISH BY
JUDITH KERMAN

WITH AN INTRODUCTION BY
LINDA M. RODRÍGUEZ GUGLIELMONI
AND JUDITH KERMAN

BOA EDITIONS, LTD. ❖ ROCHESTER, NY ❖ 2009

First Edition
09 10 11 12 7 6 5 4 3 2 1

For information about permission to reuse any material from this book, please contact The Permissions Company at www.permissionscompany.com or e-mail permdude@eclipse.net.

Publications by BOA Editions, Ltd.—a not-for-profit corporation under section 501 (c) (3) of the United States Internal Revenue Code—are made possible with funds from a variety of sources, including public funds from the New York State Council on the Arts, a state agency; the Literature Program of the National Endowment for the Arts; the County of Monroe, NY; the Lannan Foundation for support of the Lannan Translations Selection Series; the Sonia Raiziss Giop Charitable Foundation; the Mary S. Mulligan Charitable Trust; the Rochester Area Community Foundation; the Arts & Cultural Council for Greater Rochester; the Steeple-Jack Fund; the Ames-Amzalak Memorial Trust in memory of Henry Ames, Semon Amzalak and Dan Amzalak; and contributions from many individuals nationwide.

Cover Design: Sandy Knight
Cover Art: "Hermanas de Sangre III" by Belkis Ramírez
Interior Design and Composition: Richard Foerster
Manufacturing: BookMobile
BOA Logo: Mirko

Library of Congress Cataloging-in-Publication Data

Praises & offenses : three women poets from the Dominican Republic / Aída Cartagena Portalatín, Ángela Hernández Núñez, Ylonka Nacidit-Perdomo ; translated by Judith Kerman. — 1st ed.
     p. cm.
English and Spanish. Includes bibliographical references and index.
ISBN 978-1-934414-30-9 (alk. paper)
1. Dominican poetry—Women authors—Translations into English. 2. Dominican poetry—20th century—Translations into English. 3. Dominican poetry—Women authors. 4. Dominican poetry—20th century. 5. Dominican Republic—Poetry. I. Cartagena Portalatín, Aída. II. Hernández, Ángela. III. Nacidit Perdomo, Ylonca. IV. Kerman, Judith, 1945–
PQ7406.5.E5P73 2009
861'.640809287097293—dc22

                                     2009017540

BOA Editions, Ltd.
Nora A. Jones, Executive Director/Publisher
Thom Ward, Editor/Production
Peter Conners, Editor/Marketing
Bernadette Catalana, BOA Board Chair
A. Poulin, Jr., Founder (1938–1996)
250 North Goodman Street, Suite 306
Rochester, NY 14607
www.boaeditions.org

NATIONAL
ENDOWMENT
FOR THE ARTS
A great nation
deserves great art.

State of the Arts

NYSCA

Contents

❖   *Ángela Hernández Núñez*   ❖

❖   *Ylonka Nacidit-Perdomo*   ❖

Introduction

In 1492, while searching for new trading routes, Christopher Columbus' crew sighted a mountainous island, the second largest in a curving archipelago. It became the site of Spain's first colony in the New World. Soon France laid claim to its western side, and by 1795 most of the western territory officially became part of France's overseas empire. Today the Dominican Republic and the Republic of Haiti share, although uncomfortably, the island still called *La Española* or Hispaniola.

According to Francine Masiello[1], women writers under military dictatorships in Latin America have had a real concern with survival. Fear for one's life and that of family and friends, a need to be silent, a cloaking or self-censorship of one's words became deeply ingrained. Although it may be difficult for those who have grown up in democracies with civil rights to detect and understand it, strong vestiges of these feelings remain in the psyches of contemporary Latin American writers, especially women. Dominican writers such as those in this volume have hidden behind a multiplicity of masking techniques, including fragmentation and surrealism, exaggeration and doubletalk, in order to safeguard their literary enterprise and even their lives.

Aída Cartagena Portalatín, the first 20th-century woman recognized as a significant Dominican poet, began to publish in the 1940s as part of a Dominican poetry group known as the *Poesía Sorprendida*, to indicate that the poems were sudden (in the sense of the musical term *subito*) and surprising. The work of the surrealist André Breton also influenced the group.

> *La Poesía Sorprendida* ... was a reaction, on the one hand, against narrow and local nationalism, the vulgarity of decadent realism, lack of comprehension and imaginative sensibility; moreover, against rigidity and poverty of language and form resulting from ignorance of the best traditions of [the Spanish] language. On the other hand, the reaction strove against the environment of moral suffocation imposed by [Rafael] Trujillo's dictatorship. This last idea, in part, explains the predominance of symbols and metaphors as well as all sorts of ambiguous and indirect expressions, in what we may call "cloaking techniques" common to the group as a whole. This technique leaves evidence of a social protest that, expressed in some other form, would have threatened the existence of the publications, of the movement, and even of the lives of its members.[2]

Although many more women writers became visible in the 1980s, the political situation under the regime of Joaquín Balaguer remained difficult for many years. Ángela Hernández Núñez and Ylonka Nacidit-Perdomo, the younger writers in this collection, continued and in some ways extended the hermetic literary practices begun under the Trujillo dictatorship. Ester González Gimbernat, writing about the work of Hernández Núñez, points out the ways that language, fragmentation and complexity of metaphor function in these poems.

> Hernández's poems offer themselves as challenging puzzles that entice with their complexity at the same time that they promise unforeseen answers in the assembling of their parts. The initial obscurity becomes a true challenge when we confront the innumerable avenues that open each poem to multiple and inexhaustible interpretations.[3]

Gimbernat describes Nacidit-Perdomo's poetic strategy in a similar vein:

> Each reading ignites expectations that a hidden, furtive story will be revealed, and what we find is a new proposed secret or a search in a vacuum.... The poetical game with the obscurity itself, the interwoven complexity of the relationships among the unexpected images, stubbornly impedes reconstruction of a coherent enunciation, in this manner increasing the possible interpretations and even contradictions.[4]

These two poets' practices of cloaking and hermeticism, surrealism and fragmentation, while they resemble contemporary postmodern practices in Western democracies, also reflect the particular situation of women writers who grew up under the Dominican dictatorships of the 20th century. A brief reprise of Dominican political history may help to establish context.

The Early Writers and Their Historical/Social Context

Since its first days as a European colony, Hispaniola has been marked by political and social upheavals. Yet the arts flourished. Native-born authors began to write as early as the 16th century. Two of these first writers, often cited as the first poets of the New World, were women: Sor Leonor de Ovando, a Dominican nun and prioress, and Elvira de Mendoza, a wealthy woman credited with financing the construction of several important Colonial-era buildings in Santo Domingo.

Poetry has been historically so dominant in the writing of the Dominican Republic that many anthologies of Dominican literature contain no other genre. In the 18th and 19th centuries, the work of native-born Dominican women writers Manuela Aybar ("La Deana"), Josefa Antonia Perdomo, and Salomé Ureña Henríquez explored social and political topics such as Spain's colonial rule and the corruption that had begun to take over the island's government. Ureña's patriotic poetry contributed to the emergence of Dominican national consciousness during the struggles with Spain and Haiti.

Beginning in the 18th century, France and then Haiti frequently intervened in the Dominican Republic. Haitian armies occupied the Dominican Republic from 1821 to 1844, when the Dominican national movement led by Juan Pablo Duarte succeeded in driving them out.

Although the majority of Dominicans have African ancestry, the historical animosity between Haiti and the Dominican Republic played a major part in Dominican attitudes toward race and skin color. As in most Caribbean nations, the upper classes were the most obviously Caucasian, and the poorest most obviously descended from Africans, but racial attitudes were, and continue to be, more nuanced than those of the continental United States.

After 1844, political and economic unrest and successive rule by a series of *caudillos* (strong men) led to such chaos that, from 1861 to 1865, the Dominican Republic once more became a Spanish colony at the invitation of the Dominican upper classes. Typically, the groups in power would inflate the currency, send money abroad, and then leave the country when things fell apart.

Ulises Heureaux, who came to power in 1882, achieved political stability and economic modernization using brutal methods. He was finally assassinated. This was not the last time a Dominican leader would conclude that national development was only achievable by means of tight control, fear, and a complete dictatorial system.[5]

Continued political and economic instability followed Heureaux's death. Beginning in 1905, President Theodore Roosevelt involved the U.S. in the supervision of the Dominican foreign debt to forestall potential European intervention. In 1916, the United States occupied the Republic, ostensibly to protect the Panama Canal from German attack. When the U.S. revamped the land titles system, North American sugar companies increased their holdings; armed Dominican resistance groups called *gavilleros* began to form.

The United States left in 1924, leaving in place the *guardias*, military forces trained and equipped by the United States Marines. Rafael Trujillo gained control of the *guardias* and the government by 1930. A famously brutal and corrupt dictator, he greatly modernized the country, enhancing the power and wealth of his family. Trujillo promulgated the official view that all Dominicans were white, Spanish and Catholic. His policies led to the genocide of between 10,000 and 30,000 Haitians in 1937.

Trujillo's assassination in 1961 was followed by a short rule by his son Ramfis Trujillo and associate Joaquín Balaguer. The first democratic elections in 1963 were won by Juan Bosch, a well-respected writer of short fiction and social science who was a long-time opponent of Trujillo. However, only months later, Bosch was overthrown by a military coup d'état.

In 1965, President Lyndon B. Johnson sent in troops to crush a pro-Bosch, pro-constitutionalist rebellion. Joaquín Balaguer then came back to power, ruling until 1996 as a modernizing dictator known for ecological concerns. Although finally pressured into permitting democratic elections as a result of ongoing corruption scandals, he was a powerful player in the background of several unstable elected governments until his death at age 95.

This history of near constant violence and foreign intervention intertwined with radical social and economic inequality is the background to the poetry of Aída Cartagena Portalatín (1918–1994) and contemporary writers Ángela Hernández Núñez (b. 1954) and Ylonka Nacidit-Perdomo (b. 1965). Dominican literature in general attempts to engage the social realities of a nation-island which has been plagued by a particularly difficult history. In addition, Dominican writers and intellectuals have been actively involved in the politics of their nation, although this has often been dangerous.

All three of the authors in this collection have been active in political work, including feminist causes, to the extent that personal safety permitted. Although the way it is expressed in their poetry varies dramatically, all three have understood their own writing as politically engaged, reflecting social, economic, cultural and gender dilemmas of Dominican culture and history.

Aída Cartagena Portalatín

Political concern is most overt in the work of Cartagena Portalatín. She began to publish in the 1940s, when Trujillo was well into developing a machinery of absolute oppression including secret police, kidnappings (even overseas), and prisons which specialized in torture. In this period Cartagena Portalatín published the poem "Cómo llorar la muerte de una rosa" ("How to Weep for the Death of a Rose"), which asks how it is possible to mourn for the passing of a beautiful flower when people fear to mourn the death of human beings.

Cartagena Portalatín belonged to both the *Poesía Sorprendida* and to a group called *Generación del 48* (Generation of 48). The language of the *Generación del 48* "supposes no easy system of referentiality, perhaps because any overt criticism faced the obvious limit of naming the tyrant at the center of Dominican concerns."[6]

The work of this movement is marked by great social concern spurred by the decadence of the dictatorship. This group and the *Poesía Sorprendida* group represented:

> a synthesis of Dominican culture with Surrealism that undertakes to confront the oppressive regime, mainly by denying the utilitarian, "positivist" duties that Trujillo imposed on literature. . . . This movement was an artistic and sociological response against the state, the center, the father, at a time when Trujillo was all these things. . . . [Perhaps] the poets were relatively safe because the poems were so difficult that the Benefactor must have strained unsuccessfully to understand them.[7]

Later in her life, Cartagena Portalatín was active and visible at events celebrating women writers, including the *Tercer Festival de Mujeres Escritoras* (Third Festival of Woman Writers), an international conference at the National Library which took place in Santo Domingo in December 1993, organized by Nacidit-Perdomo. Six months later, when Cartagena Portalatín died, she was not yet recognized by most of the male-dominated Dominican establishment. In fact, her importance was not publicly honored until 2005, when the Santo Domingo International Book Fair was dedicated to her memory.

Cartagena Portalatín strongly wished for her work as writer, editor, and university professor to be recognized as a way of working against the aggressions of imperialism and materialism and for political and social change; her concerns were recognized by her appointment as Consul by UNESCO. Because she considered her mulatto identity central to her life and work, she even addressed the issue of racism in the U.S. in her poetry. She fought against the imposed silence of the Trujillo regime, and, in spite of the difficulties, she published five books of poetry while Trujillo was still in power.[8] After 1961, she could finally begin to express herself in a more open manner, and by 1962, when her collection *La Voz Desatada* was published, she had become much clearer in her criticism, expressing in very plain terms the fear she had felt for years as countless Dominicans were disappeared or murdered. In her poem "Elegía para las Elegías" ("Elegy for Elegies"), she wrote: "Our national history has nothing in common / with the history of happiness. / Almost all Dominican rulers / were gestated with material from the toilet or from Hell."

Ángela Hernández Núñez and Ylonka Nacidit-Perdomo

Even though the decade of the 1970s brought little political stability to the Dominican Republic, artistic and intellectual circles began a process of renewal that continues even to this day. During the 1980s and 1990s a true artistic boom began to develop. The work of Hernández Núñez and Nacidit-Perdomo, in particular, continues to explore concerns that have been suppressed by official history, while also developing other themes and modalities, such as the fantastic and erotic.

Both Hernández Núñez and Nacidit-Perdomo were born into and grew up in the repressive environment of a military government headed by Joaquín Balaguer, the blind but all-seeing president who ruled until 1996. For decades he was an adviser to Trujillo; when Trujillo was assassinated, Balaguer fled the island, then returned and managed to get himself appointed President. Hernández Núñez's poem "Tifus" ("Fever") echoes Shakespeare's *Julius Caesar*: "Sometimes I see a white shirt, / young beggars stab it." The white, magnificent toga symbolic of near-godly power has turned into a businesslike white shirt, and the Roman senators have turned into glue-sniffing street beggars. The poem's ending, "full of clarity / he endures," evokes the crafty nearly-blind politician who, above all, endured, remaining the power behind Dominican politics until his death.

Both Hernández Núñez and Nacidit-Perdomo are active in literary circles promoting the work of women writers and freedom of expression in the Caribbean. Nacidit-Perdomo was one of the group that met in 1992 in Curaçao which later became the Association of Caribbean Women Writers and Scholars. In addition, she organized women's conferences from the position she held at the National Library. Then for several years, she worked for the Ministry of Women's Affairs (*Centro de Documentación y Género de la Secretaría de Estado de la Mujer*), promoting the publication and visibility of literature by Dominican women, among other responsibilities. When there was a change of government in 2004, she lost that position because she refused to openly back one candidate or another. Most other artists had given in and signed a document supporting one candidate or another and the lists of artists' names were published in the newspapers.

Hernández Núñez participated in behind-closed-doors literary meetings or *Tertulias* held in Santo Domingo in the 1990s in honor of the writer and ex-President Juan Bosch. From 1990 to 2007, these meetings provided a rare forum for the Dominican liberal intelligentsia.

In spite of their personal actions, the poetry of Nacidit-Perdomo and Hernández Núñez can be difficult to read as overtly political. Although the poets of the 1990s did not have to fear torture and death, as Cartagena Portalatín had, open feminist activity, even on the literary front, still required personal courage in Dominican society. For both of the younger poets, as for many Caribbean women, gaining full access to their poetic voice has been difficult.

Gimbernat's comment about the poetry of Hernández Núñez clearly applies to Nacidit-Perdomo's work as well.

> Although the author knows that she is working with a "mortgaged imagina-tion"[9]... she is impelled to a practice of challenge, one in which the discourse of the traditionally feminine, of the victim, of suffering and tears, the dis-course for causes of all kinds, is left without a locatable place among the verses, creating a territory of hints and traces, crossed out and erased and nevertheless hieroglyphic writings which open into the resemanticization of multiple interpretations.[10]

Gimbernat's analysis suggests some of the reasons that both overtly political discourse and the image of the *Llorona*, the emblematic "weeping woman" of Spanish culture, are missing from these poems. Yet the metaphors all three poets employ in this collection share numerous masked references to the oppressive-ness of their social experience. Cartagena Portalatín's book title, *La Tierra Escrita: Elegías (The Written Earth: Elegies)*, might refer to the textuality which has become so much a subject of North American poetics. However, more careful reading of the elegies in the book reveals that the "written earth" is the cemetery in which the victims of tyranny are buried.

Similarly, many of the images in poems by Hernández Núñez evoke the sense of threat (see particularly "What I Have Is a Lung Closed like Stone"). The poems are marked by feelings of desolation, loss, and lack of control. While Balaguer was still President, Hernández Núñez wrote, "I close my mouth. / And my eyes are like those of a cat / hunting the shadow of the unknown." In another poem, Hernández Núñez walks on water, but it is a sea the color of bruises. The idea of being shipwrecked (powerful image for a writer living in a small country surrounded by the sea) appears in the work of all three writ-ers—an image of desolation, deprivation, and abandonment.

Of the three poets in this collection, Nacidit-Perdomo may seem, at one level, the least political in her poetry. And yet, feminism has taught that the personal is politi-cal. Is Nacidit-Perdomo's song a song to Love? Is it to ART itself? From Emma

Goldman to Che Guevara to bell hooks[11], thinkers about revolution have said that to love is the ultimate, most difficult and revolutionary act. The voice in Nacidit-Perdomo's poetry is left to wander alone and desolate in a city where she can react but not effectively lead, even in a love relationship.

Love is an agent of change but can only be achieved after many other tasks have been achieved. In the last stanza of "your name," Nacidit-Perdomo writes: *"March 10*—it is certain that you are the poetry in the poem." Has she turned completely away from any "practical" uses of poetry, as Trujillo had wanted and most tyrants require? It might seem so when she titles a poem "words please me."

Yet, is this not political? Nacidit-Perdomo, at one level, seems to say that she wears the mask of the actor, writing poetry while she has to make a living, "singing while I act to win." But perhaps she struggles to win something larger than just her everyday needs. All three poets refer in their work to the problem of self-expression and identity, and all three wrestle with the question of how their work will be seen by others, whether these evaluations be political, gender-related, or aesthetic. It is only through the self-reflective process of poetry that the poet can find the true self hidden behind the mask, "*detrás de mi yo*." Only in this secret space can the real freedom of the individual be achieved.

—Linda M. Rodríguez Guglielmoni
(University of Puerto Rico-Mayagüez)

—Judith Kerman
(Saginaw Valley State University, Michigan)

Notes to the Introduction

[1] Francine Masiello, "Discurso de mujeres, lenguaje del poder: reflexiones sobre la crítica feminista a mediados de la década del 80," *Hispamérica* 45 (1986): 57.

[2] Manuel Rueda and Lupo Hernández Rueda, *Antología Panorámica de la poesía Dominicana.* (Santo Domingo, D.R.: Ediciones de la Universidad Católica Madre y Maestra, printed by Editora del Caribe, 1972): 126 and 127. Translated by LMRG.

[3] Ester González Gimbernat, *La Poesía de Mujeres Dominicanas a Fines del Siglo XX.* (Lewiston, NY: Edwin Mellen Press, 2002): 146. Translated by JK.

[4] Gimbernat: 154.

[5] Howard J. Wiarda and Michael J. Kryzanek, *The Dominican Republic: A Caribbean Crucible,* 2nd ed. (Boulder: West View Press, 1982): 31.

[6] Doris Sommer and Esteban Torres, "Dominican Republic," *Handbook of Latin American Literature.* (New York: Garland Publishing, 1987): 253.

[7] Sommer and Torres: 256.

[8] *Víspera del sueño* (Ciudad Trujillo, Ediciones de La Poesía Sorprendida, Colección "El desvelado solitario," 1944); *Del sueño al mundo* (Ciudad Trujillo, Ediciones de La Poesía Sorprendida, Colección "El desvelado solitario," 1945); *Llámale verde* (Ciudad Trujillo, Ediciones de La Poesía Sorprendida, Colección "El desvelado solitario," 1945); *Mi mundo el mar* (Ciudad Trujillo, Colección "La isla necesaria," Núm. 2, Ed. Stella, 1953); *José Vela Zanetti* (arte monografía; Ciudad Trujillo, Colección "La isla necesaria," Núm. 6, Ed. Stella, 1954); *Una mujer está sola* (Ciudad Trujillo, Colección "La isla necesaria," Núm. 9, Ed. Stella, 1955).

[9] The idea of "mortgaged imagination," found in the work of Diana Bellesi and Francine Masiello, among others, refers to the problem women from colonized cultures have in creating an authentic literature when forced by historical circumstances to use the symbolic resources of the cultures that oppress them. Cf. Frances Masiello, *The Art of Transition: Latin American Culture and Neoliberal Crisis.* (Durham, NC: Duke University Press, 2001): 122.

[10] Gimbernat: 151.

[11] bell hooks, "Love as the Practice of Freedom." *Outlaw Culture: Resisting Representations.* (New York: Routledge Classics, 2006): 243–50.

Aída Cartagena Portalatín

Víspera del sueño

Por algo yo soy yo
y no otro. Nietzsche.

Ahora va de viaje. ¡Qué no regrese
nunca a la rémula
orilla donde viven sus ojos!

TIERRA se hará silencio,
risa no harán los hombres para que me haga eterna,
llanto no harán las piedras para que me haga arena.
Mi sangre se ha herido y se parece al fuego;
abísmate en olvido, sueño alma tu sueño,
la luz es sólo sombra,
es víspera del sueño.

Nieve se irá al cielo y vestirá la luna.
Se talarán los bosques para que la desnuden.
Sabrá a dulzura la raíz de la hierba.
Amor:
los ojos de la luz quemarán sus pestañas;
te soñaré a mi lado,
es víspera del sueño.

Mundos de pies cansados
descansarán. La sed de los recuerdos
tendrá lluvia de olvido.
Mi lecho se hará muelle sobre los cardos agrios;
soñaré con espigas,
es víspera del sueño.

Bocas querrán hablar
y no tendrán palabras.
Las piedras tendrán lenguas,
la arruga de la arena será tapiz de algas;
los mares serán mármoles;

The Eve of the Dream

Now you go journeying. Never go back
to that loathsome
shore where your eyes live!

EARTH will turn to silence,
men won't laugh to make me eternal,
stones won't cry to turn me into sand.
My wounded blood seems like fire;
sink into forgetting; I dream, soul, your dream,
the light is just shadow,
it's the eve of the dream.

Snow will ascend and garb the moon.
Forests will be stripped to make it naked.
The roots of the grass will taste sweet.
Love:
the light's eyes will burn their lashes;
I'll dream you at my side,
it's the eve of the dream.

Worlds of tired feet
will rest. Memory's thirst
will have the rain of forgetting.
My bed will be soft on the thistles;
I'll dream of seedheads,
it's the eve of the dream.

Mouths will want to speak
and will have no words.
Stones will have tongues,
the rumpled sand will be seaweed brocade;
the seas will be marble;

soñaré en sus costales,
es víspera del sueño.

El Tiempo
desde el cuerpo del Sol
con temblor de ceniza
ha reído a los hombres.
Cielos, mares, tierras.
Nacer, vivir, morir.
Los astros tienen sueño,
soñaré con los astros:
es víspera del sueño.

I'll sleep in their folds,
it's the eve of the dream.

From the body of the Sun
Time
has laughed at men
with a shiver of ashes.
Skies, seas, lands.
To be born, to live, to die.
The stars are sleepy,
I'll dream of the stars:
it's the eve of the dream.

Poema de tu olvido

EL alma en una mansión de nieve,
el traje de la palabra dejó desnuda la ausencia
y tu nombre era innombrable,
porque había naufragado
en la playa de unos labios desiertos.

Poem of Your Oblivion

THE soul in a mansion of snow,
the garment of words left absence naked
and your name became unnameable,
shipwrecked
on the sands of forsaken lips.

Del sueño al mundo

Yo poblaré para mil años
los sueños de los hombres

Vicente Huidobro-Altazor

...voy a doblar hacia esas corrientes
que se entran lentísimas en la
inmovilidad de los mares sin olas y
los cielos paralizados.

Rafael Alberti

DEL sueño al Mundo, con un Mundo en los ojos
que me ha dado mi sueño.
Con párpados abiertos en las dalias que nacen
los dedos inmóviles en las aguas rendidas.

Una estrella es una vida eterna.
Estaré junto a tí Mundo de tantos sueños,
para acallar en tu rostro, de tierra, agua y aire,
recuerdos de recuerdos...

Estarás en mi sueño como marco de un puerto.
Seré cielo con cabellera de luz
en carne de tu atmósfera.
Grabaré en la retina los Salmos
para darte las voces de los Cantos Mayores.

El viento, solista del espacio, tórnase a veces lobo.
Disfrazaré tu grito con hipérbolas raras,
secreto entendimiento sin agonias.
Te daré la alborada y el Canto del crepúsculo gris.

Con palabra primera digo
tu frente, de tiempo.
Cuando no habías nacido y fuistes variable
luna, sol, un mar que huía sin rumbo,

From the Dream to the World

For a thousand years, I will people
the dreams of men.

Vicente Huidobro-Altazor

...I will bend before these currents
which enter so slowly into the stillness
of the waveless seas and
the paralyzed skies.

Rafael Alberti

FROM the dream to the World, a World in my eyes
which my dream has given me.
With the open eyelids of the dahlias that bear
motionless fingers in the yielding waters.

A star is eternal life.
I will be close to you, World of so many dreams,
be silenced in your countenance, of earth, water and air,
memories of memories...

You will be in my dream like the enclosure of a harbor.
You will be heaven with tresses of light
incarnate in your atmosphere.
I will carve the Psalms behind your eyes
to give you the voices of the Great Cantos.

Sometimes the wind, soloist of space, becomes a wolf.
I will disguise your shout with rare exaggerations,
secret understanding without agony.
I will give you the dawn song and the Canto of gray twilight.

With my first word I speak
your brow, of time.
When you were not born and were mutable
moon, sun, a sea which fled trackless,

tal vez era esta mano, sin imagen ni sentido,
un soplo
deteniendo inconsciente las manecillas de un reloj
de espacios
y de unas horas que no retornarían...

No estoy rendida al sueño, pero inclínome al sueño
para soñarte Mundo, como te vé el silencio.
Y es sagitario el viento,
es conversar de luz la vecindad de estrellas,
es el Amor la Vida.

Y tú, tierra, despiertas,
creces y te levantas a unos ámbitos únicos,
con las formas más raras que me ha dado mi sueño.

perhaps it was this hand, imageless and senseless,
a breath
thoughtlessly holding back the hands of the clock
spaces
and hours which could never come again...

I have not surrendered to the dream, but I incline toward the dream
so I can dream you, World, as the silence sees you.
And the wind is an archer,
the region of the stars a conversation of light,
Life is Love.

And you, earth, awaken,
grow and raise yourself to some new horizon,
in the rarest of the forms my dream has given me.

Cómo llorar la muerte de una rosa

*De todos los hombres que
están vivos, ¿quién sabe algo?*
—Eclesiástes

¿CÓMO llorar la muerte de una rosa,
si los amaneceres han desdoblado el Mundo,
y en la hierba que tiembla cerca de los rosales
se han quedado las albas vueltas gotas de agua?

Sólo desde la tierra
tienen brillo de ámbar las estrellas.
A la tierra amarga vuelva
la lluvia del color de los rosales.

Sentir como los musgos se asen a las piedras;
¡hay un rencor en la brisa viajera!

Hombres no han llorado
porque caen los hombres.
¿Cómo llorar la muerte de una rosa?

How to Weep for the Death of a Rose

*Of all men living, which of them
knows anything?*
                              —Ecclesiastes

HOW to weep for the death of a rose
if the dawns have unfolded the World,
and in the grass trembling near the rosebushes
the dawns remain, turned into drops of water?

Only from the earth
do the stars have the gleam of amber.
To the bitter earth returns
rain the color of rosebushes.

To feel how the mosses grip the stones;
there is rancor in the wandering breeze!

Men have not wept
for the fall of men.
How to weep for the death of one rose?

Una mujer está sola

UNA mujer está sola. Sola con su estatura.
Con los ojos abiertos. Con los brazos abiertos.
Con el corazón abierto como un silencio ancho.
Espera en la desesperada y desesperante noche sin perder la esperanza.
Piensa que está en el bajel almirante
con la luz más triste de la creación.
Ya izó velas y se dejó llevar por el viento del Norte
en fuga acelerada ante los ojos del amor.

Una mujer está sola. Sujetando con sueños sus sueños,
los sueños que le restan y todo el cielo de Antillas.
Seria y callada frente al mundo que es una piedra humana,
móvil, a la deriva, perdido en el sentido
de la palabra propia, de su palabra inútil.

Una mujer está sola. Piensa que ahora todo es nada
y nadie dice nada de la fiesta a el luto
de la sangre que salta, de la sangre que corre,
de la sangre que gesta o muere de la muerte.

Nadie se adelanta ofreciéndole un traje
para vestir su voz que desnuda solloza deletreándose.

Una mujer está sola. Siente, y su verdad se ahoga
en pensamientos que traducen lo hermoso de la rosa,
de la estrella, del amor, del hombre y de Dios.

A Woman Is Alone

A woman is alone. Alone with her stature.
With her open eyes. With her open arms.
With her heart open like a wide silence.
She waits in the desperate and despairing night without losing hope.
She thinks she is in the flagship
with the saddest light of creation.
Already she has hoisted her sails and let herself be carried by the North wind
in accelerated flight before the eyes of love.

A woman is alone. She holds her dreams fast with dreams,
the dreams that remain to her, and all the sky of the Antilles.
Solemn and quiet before the world that is a human stone,
in motion, adrift, lost in the sense
of its own word, its useless word.

A woman is alone. She thinks that now everything is nothing
and no one says anything from the party to the mourning
about the blood that leaps, about the blood that runs
about the blood that is born or dies of death.

Nobody comes forward to offer her a dress
to clothe her voice that sobs naked, spelling itself.

A woman is alone. She feels, and her truth drowns
in thoughts that translate the beauty of the rose,
of the star, of love, of man and of God.

Tal vez inútil súplica

I

    TRATO de hacerme comprender
que lo que tenemos aquí
bajo los techos
no son campos de amor.
No quiero discutirlo.
Es mejor que me ausente
y me aleje muy lejos
de las explicaciones
para no oír la voz
que endurece a los hombres.

Dios grande y servidor:
¡deja que no la oiga!
Protégeme en el bastión
de la concordia
y cuídame allí dormida
después de haber sufrido
el último pensamiento ajeno.

Dios grande y servidor:
resta la angustia
a los atormentados
y ayúdame a escoger
a los más puros,
así, tan repentinamente
como nace la vida
en el cuerpo.

Maybe a Useless Petition

I

      I TRY to make myself understand
that what we have here
beneath the roofs
are not fields of love.
I don't want to discuss it.
It's better to leave,
go very far away
from explanations
so I won't hear the voice
that hardens men.

Great and humble God,
let me stop hearing it!
Protect me in the fortress
of harmony
and watch over me there, asleep
after suffering
the last contrary thought.

Great and humble God,
take away the anguish
of the tormented
and help me to choose
the purest ones
this way, just as suddenly
as life enters
the body.

2

Tarde, mañana y a mediodía
clamo por el ejercicio de pensar
como piensan los justos.

Desplázame, Señor, ríndeme,
no quiero aguardar en la silla
con estos pensamientos.
Tengo el temor de los ojos abiertos,
de ver filas de hombres
bajados mediante sogas,
colgados inertes,
de espaldas a la bienaventuranza,
y que mis ojos, duros como el pedernal,
acechando, espiando sus momentos,
aguarden temerosos
de verlos caer en la muerte.

3

Ayúdame para que el sueño
tenga razón en mi camastro.
Para que los hombres tengan
explicaciones en mi conciencia.
Que el casco del animal se levante
y pise su propia cabeza.
Que el hueso de una voz
adelgase la ofensa.
Que desaparezcan del Universo
las cosas que nunca se recobran.
Que el amor sea
más alto que los hombres.

2

Afternoon, morning and noon
I plead for the chance to think
as the righteous think.

Move me, Lord, subdue me,
I don't wish to wait in this chair
with these thoughts.
I am afraid of opening my eyes,
of seeing rows of men
hanging from ropes,
inert,
their backs to felicity,
and that my eyes, hard as flint,
lying in ambush, spying on their moments,
wait fearfully
to see them fall into death.

3

Help me so the dream
might be right as I lie on my mattress.
So that men might have
explanations in my conscience.
That an animal's hoof might rise up
and step on its own head.
That the skeletal voice
might lose the flesh of offense.
That those things never recovered
might disappear from the Universe.
That love might be
higher than men.

4

      Vuelve, Señor, que la vida juega
a la Muerte.
Que el Diablo juega
al Infierno.
Que el mundo juega
a la Nada.
Y procura que todo sea
como cuando era un juguete
enterrar en los surcos
un grano y otro grano
y se esperaba abundancia
para los semejantes.

4

      Return, Lord, for life plays
at Death.
The Devil plays
at Hell.
The world plays
at Nothingness.
And let everything be as it was
when it was a game
to bury in the furrows
one grain and another grain
and we hoped for abundance
for our fellow creatures.

Elegía para las Elegías

¡AY!, SIEMPRE ESTABAN LOS DOS, SE QUEDABAN
                              los dos.
Yo leía en la alcoba sentada sobre el borde del lecho.
Abrumada en largas consideraciones.
Pensaba que las cosas me golpeaban con sus puños
                                        invisibles,
hasta rendirme a mitad de unos discursos silenciosos,
cuando el sueño se filtraba por mis poros invalidando
                                mi conciencia.
Juntos más de tres décadas.

"¡Cristo!" —clamó ELLA. Fue su palabra última.

Ese tipo de recuerdo y de conversación fue anoche
entre mi padre y yo. Lo demás quedó en un monólogo
cuyas palabras corren sordas dentro de mi cabeza.
Todo el silencio son estas Elegías
donde encontrarán ofensas y alabanzas
en contra y a favor
de amados difuntos familiares,
de nacionales difuntos
y de algunos amigos.
Señores que lograron el legítimo título
de partes iguales repartidas a todos los hombres
                              la Tierra.

Elegy for Elegies

AY! THERE WERE ALWAYS TWO WHO REMAINED,
$\qquad\qquad\qquad$ those two.
I was reading in the alcove seated on the edge of the couch.
Befogged by great concerns.
I thought things were hitting me with their invisible
$\qquad\qquad\qquad\qquad\qquad$ fists,
I almost surrendered among silent conversations,
when the dream filtered into my pores, invalidating
$\qquad\qquad\qquad\qquad$ my conscience.
Together more than three decades.

"Christ!" SHE cried out. It was her last word.

This kind of memory and conversation took place last night
between my father and me. The rest remained a monologue
whose words run silently inside my head.
These Elegies are all the silence
where praises and offenses can be found
opposed and in favor
of beloved dead relatives,
of dead militiamen
and of some friends.
Gentlemen who achieved legitimate title
to equal shares dealt out to all men
$\qquad\qquad\qquad\qquad$ the Earth.

ENTREMOS MÁS A FONDO. Exploremos los detalles
de dos muchachos vírgenes
que daban la impresión de no sufrir ni gozar
y carecer de cualquier dignidad. Ese estado de más acá,
de menos o más allá, se esfumó el día que el menos idiota
descubrió que la muerte le llegaría a su madre
                              por una herida diabética.
El pobre virgen vivía una asfixiante atmósfera.
Después de comerse lo que encontraba en el plato
y un poco de las uñas, eructaba al preguntar:
                              —¿Qué es un americano?
Se reía parejo con los cabellos, los ojos, los brazos
                              y las piernas
saltando como un pájaro roto.
Era un idiota cómodo. El mismo se daba la respuesta:
—Un americano es medio millón de muertos en Nagasaki o Hiroshima.

Si repasamos los diversos periódicos y revistas que se publican
éstos expresan una desilución. Nadie escribió una letra.

Murió el de menos sexo, el de actitud de tonto rompedor
                              de platos,
con virtudes de una época próxima-futura,
como se muere cuando se es republicano-nacionalista
y espíritu libre con ciertas medallas subversivas.
Ese Erasmes era un idiota. Un virgen. No podía ser más
                              juicioso,
ni más idiota, ni más enfermo, porque su enfermedad
era ser claro. Hablar tanto de éste no es una excusa
                              para olvidar a otros.
Los González—por ejemplo—tuvieron suerte para la
                              trampa,
ya en negocios o en política sucia,
de buena o mala fe lograron el millón.
Debidamente con aspecto avergonzado murió primero uno,
después murió el otro.
En la azotea del cielo Cristo juntó a todos los pordioseros
que pidieron limosna a esos señores.

LET US GO DEEPER. Let's explore the details
of two naïve kids
who seemed to neither suffer nor enjoy
and lacked all dignity. This state of nearer to here,
of more or less there, faded away the day when the less idiotic
discovered that death had reached his mother
                                    through a diabetic wound.
The poor virgin lived in a smothering atmosphere.
After eating what he found on the plate
and a little of his fingernails, he belched, then asked:
                        —What is an American?
He laughed, his hair, his eyes, his arms
                                    and his legs
jumping like a broken bird.
He was a comfortable idiot. He gave himself the answer:
—An American is half a million dead in Nagasaki or Hiroshima.

If we scan the various newspapers and magazines in publication
they reveal disappointment. No one has written a word.

The one with less virility is dead, the one with the attitude of a stupid
                                    plate-smasher,
with the virtues of a near-future time,
the way someone dies when he is a republican-nationalist,
a free spirit with certain subversive medals.
This Erasmus was an idiot. A virgin. He could not have been more
                                    judicious,
or more idiotic, or sicker, because his sickness
was clarity. To speak this way about one is no excuse
                        for forgetting others.
The Gonzálezes—for example—were lucky with
                                    trickery,
and also in business and dirty politics,
in good or bad faith earned their million.
Eventually, shamefaced, first one died,
then the other died.
On the terrace of the heavens Christ joined all the pious beggars
who had asked these gentlemen for alms.

"—¡Cierra la boca Cristo! tú sabes que eran dos
matarratas".

El que tal así dijo murió por accidente.
Una bala le acarició amorosa la nariz curvada,
otra bala le partió el corazón en cien.
Esos mendigos fueron civiles de Moca. Uno cayó
pidiéndole a Lilís.

"—Shut your mouth, Christ! you know these two were
                                          rat-killers."

The one who spoke this way died by accident.
A bullet lovingly caressed his curved nose,
another bullet broke his heart into a hundred pieces.
These beggars were citizens of Moca[1]. One fell
asking Lilís[2] for alms.

ME OTORGO LICENCIA porque este es un libro que
                                    ilustra algunos aspectos
de la decadencia de las últimas décadas.
Observemos como un entierro evoca la existencia vacía
de ricos turistas.
Ahora esa comunicación establecida entre tu conciencia
                                    y la mía
teje una trama odiosa de antiguos recuerdos perpetuados
en este país que se derrumba o nace.
Todos esos muchachos que matan definen como un canto
                                    funeral
la HISTORIA DOMINICANA hasta el 30 de Mayo de 1961.
Habría que hacer una sola reserva: Estas Elegías
                                    desesperadas
posiblemente se bailen en una taberna de militares honestos
en el Año 2000.
Nuestra historia nacional no tiene nada en común
con la historia de la felicidad.
A casi todos los gobernantes dominicanos
los gestaron con material de excusado y del Infierno.

El espíritu del benemérito Juan Pablo no nació mellizo.
Tontos y carajos dijeron que el nacimiento de algunos personajes
—tiranos, autoritarios, demagogos, lampiños o barbudos,
cuyos retratos decoran los libros de textos— era cosa de predestinados.
Así se definen algunos proyectos
que los niños de las escuelas aprenden de memoria.

AYER A LA DIEZ visité el cementerio con dos niñas.
Es un deber de amor de lo más cruel.
Las niñas que no saben cuánto cuesta la muerte
se entusiasmaron mirando "las casitas donde viven los muertos".
—Ah, —dijo una— ¡qué lindas para jugar muñecas!
Era un cementerio planificado:
Calles—árboles recortados—flores—tres jardineros—
seis policías—dos porteros—cuatro enterradores—albañiles
—varias prostitutas buscando su comercio—agua—luz—

I GIVE MYSELF PERMISSION because this is a book that

illustrates some aspects

of the decadence of the last few decades.

We see how a funeral evokes the empty existence

of rich tourists.

Now this communication established between your conscience

and mine

weaves a hateful fabric of old memories kept alive

in this land which is crumbling or being born.

All these fellows who killed defined as a funeral

march

DOMINICAN HISTORY before the 30th of May, 1961.

Only one reservation would be necessary: These desperate

Elegies

might dance in a tavern of honest soldiers

in the Year 2000.

Our national history has nothing in common

with the history of happiness.

Almost all Dominican rulers

were gestated with material from the toilet or from Hell.

The spirit of the worthy Juan Pablo[3] did not produce a twin.

Idiots and pricks said that the birth of some people

—tyrants, authoritarians, demagogues, barefaced or bearded,

whose portraits decorate our textbooks—was foreordained.

That is how some projects defined themselves

for schoolchildren to memorize.

YESTERDAY AT TEN A.M., I visited the cemetery with two girls,

a debt of love of the cruelest kind.

The girls who don't know how much death costs

cheerfully admired "the little houses where the dead live."

—Ah!—said one—what pretty places to play with dolls!

It was a planned cemetery:

Streets—trimmed trees—flowers—three gardeners—

six policemen—two porters—four gravediggers—stonemasons

—several prostitutes looking for business—water—light—

teléfono—un administrador—escribientes, sanitarios en
diferentes partes dispuestos...
Un cementerio es una oficina de Relaciones Públicas
para negociar la última tierra.
Pobres y ricos: ¡¡todos muertos!!
Nombres y fechas. ESA ES LA TIERRA ESCRITA.

telephone booth—an administrator—writers, bathrooms
in various locations...
A cemetery is a Public Relations office
for the business of the last piece of turf.
Poor and rich: all dead!!
Names and dates. THIS IS THE WRITTEN EARTH.

DESPUÉS DE UN ENCANTAMIENTO LÍRICO llega el
segundo movimiento
Que sea la conciliación de la llama que destruye
Finalmente la prosa común o el extracto de una lacrimógena.
Pensemos en la unión para entrar en otras ELEGÍAS.
Que sea la conciliación de la llama que destruye
con la rosa de luz creciendo en esta segunda parte
del Siglo de Lenin, McArthur, Hitler, Churchill, Kruschev,
Kennedy, Juan XXIII, y además A B C D E F G H I J K
L M N O P Q R S T U V W X Y Z...

ANTES DE RESPONDER a lo que opina el lector
                                   de mis nuevos poemas,
yo pretendí hablar con dignidad y elegancia, al centro,
y unir los pensamientos que tuvieron los muertos.

AFTER A LYRICAL ENCHANTMENT comes the
second movement
The reconciliation of the flame that destroys
At last common prose or the abstract of tears.
Let's think about that union, to enter other ELEGIES.
The reconciliation of the flame that destroys
with the rose pink of growing light in this second part
of the Century of Lenin, MacArthur, Hitler, Churchill, Khrushchev,
Kennedy, John XXIII, and also A B C D E F G H I J K
L M N O P Q R S T U V W X Y Z...

BEFORE RESPONDING to the reader's opinion
                              of my new poems,
I aim to speak with dignity and elegance, to get to the heart of things,
and make one composition of the thoughts of the dead.

Elegía Segunda

MI MADRE FUE UNA DE LAS GRANDES MAMÁ
                              del mundo.
De su vientre nacieron siete hijos
que serían en Dallas, Menphis o Birminghan un
                                   problema racial.
(Ni blancos ni negros.)
Lala al servicio de la casa por más de treinta años no la olvida.
En cada frío que se hace en nuestro valle
la recuerdan también los que recibieron en el pueblo sus frazadas baratas.
Mamá ignoraba las Teorías Políticas. (Encíclicas y a Marx.)
Sólo entendía que el pobre sufre hambre, reclama pan y
                                   necesita abrigo.
Un periodista dijo que ella era un programa privado
                    de Asistencia Social.
Mujeres de vida buena y de vida mala aun la lloran.
Sus cosas eran deber de amor.

Mamá. Olimpia. Mamá. El público no debe por fundas de alimentos
ni frazadas y techos
levantar estatuas. Deber de amor son esas cosas.
Deber del hombre por todos los HOMBRES.

Second Elegy

MY MOTHER WAS ONE OF THE GREAT MAMAS
                              of the world.
Seven children were born from her belly
who in Dallas, Memphis or Birmingham would have been a
                              racial problem.
(Neither whites nor blacks.)
Lala serving in the house for more than 30 years does not forget her.
With every cold snap that comes to our valley
they remember her, those among the people
who received her cheap blankets.
Mama ignored Political Theory (Encyclicals and Marx).
She only understood that the poor suffer hunger, cry for bread
                              and need a coat.
A journalist said that she was a private
                              Social Welfare program.
Women who lived good lives and even bad lives cried for her.
Her concerns were labors of love.

Mama. Olympia. Mama. The public shouldn't put up statues
for bags of food
or blankets and roofs. These things were a duty of love.
The duty of everyone toward EVERYONE.

¡POBRE NEGRA la niñera! Mi casa era un circo.
(Pelotas, muñecas, columpios, patines, gritos, castigos y
vainas.)
Durante diez años Negra tendió sobre mi cuerpo
la sabanita blanca.

(¡QUE DIOS HAYA REPARTIDO CON ELLA EL
LATIFUNDIO DE SU REINO, Y QUE DESCANSE
EN PAZ!!!!)

Porque luego la Negra corrió con muchos varones en
Curazao.
Más, es necesario que hable de élla con AMOR
ADMIRACIÓN
DIGNIDAD
porque cuando cuidó mi infancia
su vida estaba pura de respeto
y llena de renunciamientos.
Para buscar el sueño yo unía mi pensamiento al suyo
y su silencio al mío.
Ahora los brazos de mi soledad se extienden como alambres
hacia su recuerdo. De todos modos:
¡NEGRA!, ¡NEGRA!, muy alto grito: ¡¡¡NEGRA!!!

Negra muerta: te digo en esta página
que, a veces, el recuerdo de un muerto es pesado e indigesto.
—Lo cierto es—me explicó un psiquiatra—
que el recuerdo para ser correctamente asimilado
necesita estar pegado a un sentimiento de amor, gratitud,
admiración, odio, sexo, o cualquier otro tema...

POOR NEGRA, my black nursemaid! My house was a circus.
(Balls, dolls, seesaws, skates, shouts, punishments and

                                                            irritation.)

For ten years Negra spread over my body
                        the soft white sheet.

        (GOD GIVE HER A SHARE IN THE HOLDINGS
              OF HIS KINGDOM, AND LET HER REST
                          IN PEACE!!!!)

Because afterward Negra ran with the boys in
                        Curaçao.
But one must speak of her with LOVE
                    ADMIRATION
                    DIGNITY
because when she cared for my childhood
her life was pure with attentiveness
and full of renunciations.
To search for the dream I joined my thought with hers
and her silence with mine.
Now the arms of my solitude reach like wires
toward her memory. In any case:
NEGRA! NEGRA! I shout very loudly: NEGRA!!!

My dead Negra: I tell you on this page
that, sometimes, the memory of a dead one is heavy and undigested.
—What is certain—a psychiatrist explained to me—is
that memory to be assimilated correctly
must be bonded to a feeling of love, gratitude,
admiration, hatred, lust or some other mania...

EN MI PUEBLO DE MOCA, República Dominicana.
INDIAS OCCIDENTALES
A – M – É – R – I – C – A

(Continente de indios
mestizos
negros
blancos y
rubios.
Continente de HOMBRES
y de HAMBRE —Trópico
y flechas al Sur.)

En Moca
tenían como sabio a Cervantes, un sacerdote español
que luego se hizo médico, se casó
y su mujer le parió varios hijos.
Lo recuerdo porque una vez escribió que lo animal del
hombre
era derivado de una línea de mamíferos terrestres.
Cosa que creí hasta que Jean Marie Gerint científica
en la década sexta de este Siglo XX
que el hombre procede del mar y se acerca a la esponja
porque el 72% de su peso es AGUA.
Agua del hombre, precisamente, la que nadie ha podido
beber.

IN MY TOWN OF MOCA, Dominican Republic.
WEST INDIES
A – M – E – R – I – C – A

(Continent of Indians
                    mixed-bloods
                    blacks
                    whites and
                    blondes.
Continent of HUMANS
and of HUNGER—Tropic
arrowing to the South.)

In Moca
there was, like a wise sage in Cervantes, a Spanish priest
who became a physician, married,
and his wife bore him several children.
I remember him because once he wrote that the human animal
descended from a lineage of terrestrial mammals.
I believed that until Jean Marie Gerint, a woman scientist,
wrote in the 6th decade of this 20th Century
that humans came from the sea and are nearly sponges
because 72% of our weight is WATER.
Human water, precisely that water that no one has been able
                                                    to drink.

FREDDY MILLER un cuentista dominicano
con un nombre en inglés
murió en alta mar.
Dicen. Dijeron.
Como de sus cuentos también de su muerte se hablará
                                            mucho tiempo.

El diario de la mañana
en manos del tirano

                        dio la noticia
                        en una sección
                        que se llamaba:

```
┌─────────────────────────────────────┐
│                                     │
│           SUCESOS                   │
│                                     │
└─────────────────────────────────────┘
```

La muerte y la política continuamente se mezclaban
como el agua y la harina del pan de cada amanecer.
¡Pan amargo! Gloria. Réquiem.
Hace unos meses se pasaba revista con lujo de detalles
a una legión de muertos. Terminó la sesión
                        cuando alguien se levantó
para añadir tu nombre FREDDY.

FREDDY MILLER, a Dominican writer
with an English name,
died on the high seas.
They say. They said.
Like his stories, people will talk about his death
                                    for a long time.

The morning paper
in the hands of the tyrant

                        gave the news
                        in a section
                        called:

CURRENT EVENTS

Death and politics mix continually
like the water and flour of the morning bread.
Bitter bread! Gloria. Requiem.
A few months ago they examined in extravagant detail
a legion of dead men. The session ended
                        when someone got up
to add your name FREDDY.

ESTAMOS EN UN PUNTO neurálgico de nuestra
Historia Patria.
En que las cosas quieren SER o DEJAR DE SER
Podemos llegar a ser mucho.
O ser nada.
Algunos han consentido negociar por cualquier cosa
los esqueletos de sus muertos mancillados.
Le dieron un automóvil de lujo, una casa grande,
dinero, viajes o una buena pensión

$ A CAMBIO

de un marido, una mujer, un padre, un hermano
o de un hijo acribillado.
Y hasta por el honor de una hija que murió
abortada
entre los brazos de una comadrona clandestina.
Esto lo escribo porque es conocida esa mamá que aceptó
la tragedia
recibiendo una casa en la Calle...............Ciento doce.
Esa madre es una carajo, cogollo!!!
(No quiero deshonrar más la deshonra.)

WE ARE AT THE PAINFUL POINT of our
                              National History.
When things want TO BE or NOT TO BE
We can achieve a great deal.
Or nothing.
Some have agreed to trade for almost anything
the bones of their dishonored dead.
A luxury automobile, a big house,
money, travel or a good pension

$ TO EXCHANGE

for a husband, a wife, a father, a brother
                    or a child punctured like a sieve.
And even for the honor of a daughter who died
                              aborted
in the arms of a clandestine midwife.
I write this because it's well known that the mother who accepted
                                        the tragedy
received a house on...............One Hundred Twelfth Street.
This mother is a whore, the cream of the crop!!!
(I don't want to further disgrace the disgrace.)

PARA SABER cuánto cuesta el honor
hay que acercarse al gran inválido.
Al gran herido por el hambre y la miseria.
Después que Justina la costurera se quitó la vida
porque a Justina la violó un pelafustán.
Todas las mañanas Justina se comía a Cristo entero
en la iglesia vecina.
No pudo soportar el ultraje.
Su voz era la voz de Cristo.
El hambre de Justina era el hambre de Cristo.
La vergüenza de Justina la invalidó.
Mas, nos toca vivir en una época difícil
de encontrar otra igual en la historia del Mundo.
Gracias, Justina, yo fui testigo de tu llanto.
El satélite de ese gran mandón
olvidó que en esta Media Isla los dominicanos
asisten al entierro de los pelafustanes.

El motor que mueve la actividad decencia
tiene un botón exacto que se llama JUSTICIA.

TO KNOW how much honor costs
you have to get close to the great cripple.
The one so wounded by hunger and misery.
Justina the seamstress took her own life
after Justina was raped by a son-of-a-bitch.
Justina used to eat Christ whole
in the church next door.
She couldn't stand the outrage.
Her voice was the voice of Christ.
Justina's hunger was the hunger of Christ.
Justina's shame made her hollow.
But we find ourselves living in a time difficult
to equal in the history of the World.
Thank you, Justina, I am witness to your weeping.
The moon that orbits this great bully
forgot that on this Half Island the Dominicans
attend the burial of sons-of-bitches.

The motor that moves decency
has a starter button labeled JUSTICE.

memorias negras

tono 1.

vertical camino derribado
reducido a esencia original
fatalidad: el hombre
su problema inherente
simplemente la raza

el verbo de los ágrafos
betún de la piel negra
la cama en el pajal

el reclamo del vientre
la insistencia del sexo
responso lloro pena la nube

llueve

black memories

tone 1.

way of uprightness knocked down
reduced to its original essence
fate: man
his inherent problem
simply race

the word of the illiterate
asphalt of black skin
bed in the hayfield

the clamor of the belly
the insistent pull of sex
response   cry   grief   the cloud

it rains

memorias negras

tono 2.

OoooooooooooH
oh
negación del amor
quién habló de soledad y esperanza
llorar   llorar   llorar
no habéis la muerte preparado
llora la muerte   llora el cielo   llora el negro
oooooooh amor
        amor asesinado

black memories

tone 2.

OoooooooooooH
oh
refusal of love
who spoke of solitude and hope?
to weep   to weep   to weep
you have not prepared death
death weeps   heaven weeps   the Black man weeps
oooooooh love
        murdered love

memorias negras

tono 3.

era tanta la lluvia en *shaperville*
la nube cerró el ojo
para no verse mojar los cadáveres

era tanta la muerte en *shaperville*
la lluvia se tapó el oído
para no oirse caer sobre cadáveres

black memories

tone 3.

there was so much rain in *sharpeville*[4]
the cloud closed an eye
so it could not see itself soaking the corpses

there was so much death in *sharpeville*
the rain plugged an ear
so it could not hear itself fall on corpses

memorias negras

tono 4.

son las noticias y memorias negras
destroza el cuerpo la metralleta
        repartiendo plomos
oooooooooh

asesinando a la magnolia negra
compás a contratiempo los disparos
cobardemente asesinando a áfrica
cobardemente explotando a áfrica
ooooooh   oooooh

tres días la muerte horizontal tendida
responso lloro pena la nube

                      llueve

black memories

tone 4.

these are the bulletins and memories of blackness
firearms tear the body apart
          dealing out bullets
ooooooooh

murdering the black magnolia
the counterpoint beat of bullets
cowardly murdering Africa
cowardly exploiting Africa
ooooooh   oooooh

three days death spreading horizontally
response   weep   grief   the cloud

              it rains

memorias negras

tono 5.

shaperville
en esa tierra se llega al hambre
en esa tierra el hambre saluda el día
los plomos queman
la sangre aúlla
revelará el secreto de la memoria negra
el polvo de los huesos calcinados
        ay, ay, ay, ay
asesinaron otra vez a áfrica
otra vez en *shaperville*
ooooh   oooooh
OoooooooooooooooH
nadie grita: castigo

black memories

tone 5.

sharpeville
on this ground hunger gathers
on this ground hunger greets the day
the bullets burn
the blood howls
it will expose the secret of Black memory
the dust of burned bones
       ay, ay, ay, ay
again they murdered Africa
again in *sharpeville*
ooooh   oooooh
Ooooooooooooooooo0H
no one screams: punishment

exterminio en gris

dejarla dijeron los hijos
dejarla buscar su propia voz
con la edad de su cuerpo
con lo visto lo sentido

       decir que no encontró
            la poesía

        decir antes o después
        del exterminio en gris
        que sufre porque

fácil no   ni tan sencillo es
lanzar a un mendigo muerto
en una plaza pública
    oh desamparado
          se te pega de la piel
        el desamparo

cuando el robledal cambia toda
su hojarasca
forja el clima que prepara
otros advenimientos

puede decirse oh Dios que los que
           nada hicieron
despertaron un culto que aplastará
           la tierra

oh enemigos de la verdad y la luz
se mueve en su contra el viento
lleno de carcajadas para golpear
en los cuatro costados
el odio redoblado

extermination in gray

to leave her, the children said,
to let her find her own voice
with the age of her body
with what has been seen and sensed

        to say she did not find
              poetry

        to say before or after
        the extermination in gray
        that she suffers because

easy, no   it's not so simple
to throw out a dead beggar
in a public place
    oh abandoned
              it sticks to your skin
              the abandonment

when the oak grove changes all
its dead leaves
it forges the climate that prepares
other arrivals

it can be said oh God that those who
                  did nothing
awakened a worship that will crush
             the earth

oh enemies of truth and light
the wind moves against you
full of guffaws to strike
on four sides
redoubled hatred

los hombres y sus cálculos
moldean la desgracia
todos quieren a su favor
poseer el universo
con falsas mentiras
en rasgos ascendentes
ahí están los que aspiran a un trono en las
                                        galaxias
más allá del poder oh aventura
ese poder que aplasta
que deja que yazga horizontal
su prójimo

II

No es héroe ni nada
sólo un protagonista de sagas
                        arribistas
dante preparó todos los circulos
        para
                el
                        tránsito
de la comedia humana

que retrata *balzac*
oh inmodestia a horcajadas
oh vanidad de pie
                que espera
                los misiles
                ver los ojos
                reverberar
                al fuego
no sé para contarlo a quién...

oh desgracias creadas por el hombre
que participa en el alumbramiento

men and their calculations
shape misfortune
they all want to possess the universe
for their benefit
with false lies
in ascendant exploits
there they are, the ones that aspire to a throne in the
galaxies

beyond power oh adventure
that power that crushes
that leaves its neighbor
lying flattened

II

He's not a hero, nothing like it
only the protagonist of self-seeking sagas
dante prepared all the circles
      for
            the
                traffic
of the human comedy

that *balzac* portrays
oh immodesty astride
oh vanity standing
            who waits for
            the missiles
            to see the eyes
            echo
            with fire
I don't know whom they will tell the story...

oh misfortunes created by the man
who participates in the enlightenment

de la muerte
oh desquiciada sociedad
            que se destruye
                    sin honores
donde las cosas rigen por
                    máquinas
                    intermedias
                    o infernales
todo es temor donde solamente uno
            es el dueño del éxito

III

se oye de tanto confesarlo
al más grande de cada continente
que la p–a–z esta lista
            que está muerta
como si no estuviese ya

dios llora   no es un tonto
llora
llora   oooh
llora   cuando oye el desafío
                    en jergas tan distintas

                of death
oh unhinged society
                that destroys itself
                                without honor
where things govern by
                machines
                intermediary
                or infernal
everything is fear where only one
                is the master of success

                        III

everywhere, confessions are heard
from the greatest of every continent
that p-e-a-c-e is done
                that it is dead
as if it were not already

god weeps   he is not an idiot
weeps
weeps   oooh
weeps   when he hears the challenge
                        in such unmistakable doubletalk

Ángela Hernández Núñez

Andar Ligero

En la inocencia, la eternidad posible.

Pero he amado aprisa,
con la atención de objetos que se fugan.
Me hallo diciendo, cerrad las puertas.
Me hallo diciendo, amor deberás irte.
Me hallo tocando líneas en las piedras.

Pienso en las mujeres que esperaron,
no Ulises, sino hombres corrientes.
Aquellos que asediaron ciudades,
tras la forma inabarcable
de sus propios corazones.

He amado después y en la tormenta.
Llevo una carga de luz:
hace ceniza el aire.

To Go Lightly

In innocence, eternity is possible.

But I have loved in haste,
with the attentiveness of objects that fly away.
I find myself saying, close the doors.
I find myself saying, love you ought to leave.
I find myself touching lines in the stones.

I think about the women who waited,
not for Ulysses, but for ordinary men.
Those who laid siege to cities,
beyond the great width
of their own hearts.

I have loved after and during the storm.
I carry a burden of light:
it turns the air to ashes.

Arca Espejada

El amor ha florecido demasiado.
Cortemos el amor.
Cortemos en la cima.

La hora más difícil acontece.
Veo estirarse el aire. La lluvia irresistible.
Cierro mi boca.
Y mis ojos son como de gato vigilante,
tras el asomo de lo desconocido.

Mas la ciudad aguarda la tormenta.
Los lugares sucumben.
Fuentes perdurables crecen del crepúsculo.

Miras mi sombra, la otra superficie,
campo impuro de enigma,
donde imantas el tiempo transcurrido.

Dormir no es justo ante tantos ventanales.

Qué aúlle la inocencia.
Abrigue mi casa y la demuela.

Mirrored Casket

Love has bloomed too much.
We will prune love.
We will nip it at its peak.

The most difficult time occurs.
I see the air draw tight. The irresistible rain.
I close my mouth.
And my eyes are like those of a cat
hunting the shadow of the unknown.

But the city waits for the storm.
The villages yield.
Inexhaustible springs grow from the dusk.

You watch my shadow, another surface,
impure landscape of enigma,
where you draw to yourself times that have gone.

It is not right to sleep before so many large windows.

Let innocence howl.
Let it protect my house and demolish it.

Lividez del Paisaje

¡Horror tierno Quevedo!
Somos la espora.
Esto del mundo, ¿hacia dónde acude?
Miro correrse el diminuto frío.
Sé que me está mirando un cuerpo bello
y su horrible tristeza huele a risa.
Cerramos los ojos para iluminarnos.
Intocables son todas las cosas.
Yo, detenido marfil de las estatuas,
te concedo bailar sobre mis huesos.

The Landscape's Deathly Pallor

Tender horror, Quevedo![5]
We are the spore.
This worldliness, where did it come from?
I see the little coldness melting.
I know that it is looking at me, a handsome body
whose horrible sadness smells like laughter.
We close our eyes to illuminate ourselves.
Everything is untouchable.
I, frozen like the marble of statues,
give you permission to dance on my bones.

Reunión Conmigo

Ha florecido el patio.
Corte en la zona de mis debilidades.
Duermo con el dolor. Le soy extraña.

Es largo y desconocido el camino
de volver hacia mí.

El fuego que vieron arder mis ojos.
El agua sobre el cuerpo.
El aire sin nombre ni dirección.
La arena llena de cosas milenarias.

Mis pies han olvidado.
Y mi corazón danza bajo el látigo del amor.

Los poetas enferman como las manzanas.
Se ha borrado el lenguaje de lo eterno.
La verde primavera ríe oscura.

Que el silencio me purifique.
Que la soledad me alumbre.

Ahora soy Galatea. Anónima espora.
Tengo que morir a la servidumbre.
Olvido ser mujer. Olvido ser alguien.
Olvido la juventud y la vejez.

El mundo está espléndido.
¿Cómo pueden no verlo mis entrañas?

Meeting with Myself

The patio has bloomed.
A cut through the zone of my weaknesses.
I sleep with pain. I am a stranger to it.

The road back to myself
is long and unknown.

The fire my eyes saw as it burned.
The water on my body.
The air without name or address.
The sand full of ancient things.

My feet have forgotten.
And my heart dances under the whip of love.

The poets sicken like apples.
The language of the eternal has been erased.
The green springtime laughs darkly.

Let the silence purify me.
Let the solitude ignite me.

Now I am Galatea. Anonymous spore.
I have to die to servitude.
I forget to be a woman. I forget to be anyone.
Forget youth and old age.

The world is splendid now.
Why can't my body believe it?

Simple

Impudorosa, móvil entre dos planos,
lapido sensaciones, como arpegios.
Mojan mi espalda. *Siento* mis pupilas.

Cúpulas de hojas y ociosos reptiles,
                        graban el horizonte,
por donde abre la luz sosegadamente.

Aguas blancas, aguas azules, fluyen entre nubes.

Me conjuga el paisaje. Vive él porque lo siento.
De pirámides llena mis cuencas,
líneas las piernas,
circunferencias en el plexo.

Causa pavor lo bello que va pudriendo.

Clarea el precipicio un dilecto color amarillo.
Sale el tiempo de mi imaginación
como una cinta indescriptible.

Al fin la libertad se me muestra.
Pero es el otro brazo de la locura.

Aquilato convenciones. A su sombra pervivo.
        Sombra de árbol arenoso.

Simple

Shameless, moving between two flat surfaces,
I cut facets into feelings, like arpeggios.
They wet my back. I *feel* the pupils of my eyes.

Domes of leaves and lazy reptiles
                    carve the horizon,
where the light opens calmly.

White water, blue water, flow among clouds.

The landscape conjugates me. It lives because I feel it.
It fills my valleys with pyramids,
my legs with lines,
my solar plexus with circles.

It causes dread, the beauty that decays.

The abyss dawns, a delicious yellow color.
Time flows from my imagination
like an indecipherable ribbon.

At last liberty appears to me.
But it's the other arm of insanity.

Conventions, their value tested. In its shadow, I survive.
        Shadow of a tree full of sand.

Tifus

La taza de café se quiebra entre mis manos.
Mi mente incendia.

De las noches se desprenden semillas
y manos delincuentes.
A veces veo una camisa blanca,
jóvenes pordioseros la apuñalan.

Entre las cosas fijas, él va liviano.
Va lejos.
El cofre, la parafina, tos.
Ese algo de viejo entre la cama.
Él sale de madrugada a recoger imágenes,
de las que vienen por las aguas sucias.

Lleno de claridad,
                    perdura.

Fever

The cup of coffee breaks in my hands.
My mind catches fire.

Seeds detach from the night
and delinquent hands.
Sometimes I see a white shirt,
young beggars stab it.

Among the fixed things, he goes lightly.
He goes far.
The trunk, the paraffin, the cough.
Something of the old in bed.
He goes out before dawn to gather images,
of those who come on the dirty waters.

Full of clarity,
                    he endures.

Si quiero huir

Muerdo mis uñas:
Recuerdo obligaciones de mañana.

Si quiero odiar, miro mis garras en el agua.
Si quiero odiar, recuerdo de la palabra el poder
        cabalístico
el poder del deseo y la intención.

Si quiero dudar, sostengo en el aire mis músculos
        elásticos:
Escucho al mundo exento de mi cuerpo.

Si quiero llorar, bostezo. Tiempo y mundo acortan
        la órbita en mi ojo.
Si quiero llorar, prendo lámparas.

Si me siento en una gruta, no hay enemigos ni presa.
Si me siento en una gruta, espero el alba.

No hay escape ante tanto secreto embellecido.
Llevo estupor y asombro para el otro.
Llevo apetito y muerte.
Entre mis fauces, la lengua para lamer mis hijos
        y los dientes afilados para el perdón.

No hay escape en este ahora de agua caliente
en las narices y furia de niños.
No hay escape en este lugar sin puertas ni caminos.
Alrededor de mí la luz, el círculo infinito.

If I Want to Run Away

I bite my nails:
Remember tomorrow's obligations.

If I want to hate, I look at my claws in the water.
If I want to hate, I remember the power of the word
        cabalistic
the power of desire and intention.

If I want to doubt, I keep my elastic muscles
        aloft in the air:
I listen to the world unobstructed by my body.

If I want to cry, I yawn. Time and world shorten
        their orbit in my eye.
If I want to cry, I light lamps.

If I sit down in a cavern, there are neither enemies nor prey.
If I sit down in a cavern, I wait for the dawn.

There is no escape before such a glorified secret.
I bring stupor and fear for the other.
I carry appetite and death.
In my jaws, the tongue to lick my children
        and sharpened teeth for forgiveness.

There is no escape in this now of hot water
in the noses and fury of children.
There is no escape in this place without doors or roads.
Around me the light, the endless circle.

El orden de lo finito

Estoy soñando contigo, dice una voz en la noche.
Camino sobre un espejo lívido. Tal vez la mar.
Monstruo indefenso. Pueblo tierno de césped.
Ronronea.

En cercanía, luciérnagas, brevísimas piedras,
hunden la oscuridad.

Del otro lado surgen filamentos de hierba.
En el cielo un relámpago,
sonrisa de enigmática presencia.

Estoy soñando contigo:
Fíjate en las flores de las cañas.

Sedosas.
      Fluctuantes.
            Flotantes.

Velos en mi sangre soplados por tu boca.

Dice una voz en la noche:
Hay un grano de polvo,
un rosal que levita en nuestro patio.

The Order of the Finite

I am dreaming of you, says a voice in the night.
I walk on a mirror the color of bruises. Perhaps the sea.
Helpless monster. Tender community of lawns.
Purring.

Nearby, lightning bugs, the briefest stones,
destroy the darkness.

From the other side grow filaments of grass.
In the sky, a lightning flash,
smile of an enigmatic presence.

I am dreaming of you:
Pay attention to the flowers of the sugarcane.

Silky.
     Wavering.
          Floating.

Veils billowing in my blood at the touch of your breath.

A voice in the night says:
There's a speck of dust,
a rosebush that floats upward in our patio.

Reloj en hora

Ha pasado por llover la tierra.
Luz. Humedad.
El lagarto abraza con ternura
la espina del naranjo. Su orbe mira
y adormece.

Explayada en la blanca pared, la sombra de una mosca.

La sábila saluda al calamar con malicia.
Mariquitas en el tallo. El pino, nervio radiante,
        se estremece.

El barrer de la escoba en el patio vecino: exaltación.

Planos de árboles y anchura, láminas de un compendio:
el sendero de venir.

Distancia de las palabras. Desliz. Espacio.
¿Qué armonía se oculta?

Algo conozco que no sé que conozco.

Vuelvo mi cara. No está el lagarto, ni la mosca.
En la pared, la sombra de mi cuerpo.

Watch, Running on Time

Rain has passed over the earth.
Light. Moisture.
The lizard tenderly embraces
the thorn of the orange tree. Its orb looks around
and goes to sleep.

Cast on the white wall, the shadow of a fly.

The aloe greets the squid with malice.
Ladybugs on the stem. The pine, a radiant nerve,
      trembles.

The sweeping of a broom in the neighboring patio: exaltation.

Flat expanses of trees, pages of a compendium:
the path of arrival.

Distance of words. A slippage. Space.
What harmony hides itself?

I know something that I don't know I know.

I turn my face away. The lizard is not there, nor the fly.
On the wall, the shadow of my body.

Lo que tengo es un pulmón cerrado como piedra

Ojo móvil. Terco sobre el día vulnerable.
Ventolera. Festín de insinuaciones. Cosas de acá, de allá.
Lo que tengo es un dedo de Dios. Empuja sobre un
mismo punto de mi carne. Exige la respuesta para la
cual no hizo mis sentidos.

Lo que tengo es un punzón de siempre. De antes.
    Tajando la neblina en mis cavilaciones.
Un vestigio con forma de serpiente. Necedad de furia,
baileteo —frío de ser—.
Lo que tengo es la consciente impotencia felina.
    Oscuridad de las sacerdotisas. Clara interrogación
sobre enigmas y decantaciones. Un inútil
pedestal por hombros, navegando entre cálices,
espadas.

Lo que tengo es el vivo de los barrios.
    La culebrilla feliz de los mercados
míseros. Boca del alma rota por el vino. El tempranero
empeño de quien trueca la eternidad por alimentos.

Sueños de perseguidos —asediada—.
    Decapitados —torturada—. Suelo sobre el cuerpo sin
apoyo. Dictadura del símbolo —cara y cruz—.

Lo que tengo es el extremo de los centros.
    El comienzo. El paso y lo que pasa luego.

What I Have Is a Lung Closed like Stone

Roaming eye. Stubborn upon the vulnerable day.
Pinwheel. Feast of insinuations. Things of here, of there.
What I have is the finger of God. It keeps pushing on the same
point of my flesh. It demands an answer for which
my senses were not made.

What I have is the pinprick of always. Of the past.
    Carving the fog of my fretfulness.
A trace in the form of a serpent. Idiot fury,
clumsy jig—coldness of being—.
What I have is conscious feline impotence.
    Darkness of priestesses. Clear interrogation
about enigmas and outpourings. A useless
pedestal for shoulders, navigating between chalices,
swords.

What I have is the liveliness of the barrios.
    The happy snake dance of the wretched
markets. Mouth of the soul broken by wine. The premature
zeal of those who trade eternity for food.

Dreams of persecution—besieged—.
    Beheaded—tortured—earth upon the helpless
body. Dictatorship of the symbol—heads and tails—.

What I have is the extreme of the centers.
    The beginning. The first step and what comes next.

La física la vence una imagen

Desde el comienzo y por principio mismo
me constituyen el equilibrio y la pasión,
las enseñanzas y los imponderables

La tierra reposa su transparencia en frutos
Todo mar me resulta nostálgico
Y el amor canon suficiente

Alguna vez se unirá mi naturaleza con mi nombre
Mi corazón en alas se habrá desvanecido
Mientras tanto, no me constriñan a la imagen

No quiero ser examinada como colegial
Ni con palabras post y de modernidad
Descarto un nombre camisa de fuerza

Como el firmamento contempla a la tierra,
matriz de muerte y vida en su fecundidad y dinamismo,
así miro los cambios en mí misma
Las corrientes orgánicas me despabilan
tomo conciencia en ellas

Me aprietan los lazos y las separaciones
He conocido los regalos que cubren faltas
Y observo a la estrella desde el septentrión
avanzar hasta el afecto oceánico
El tiempo labra en mí sin sentido rarezas,
verdes instalaciones y recato

Entre las manos amadas asoma un bosque:
Hélices, velas,
atardecer de llovizna y colmillos de tigres

The Image Vanquishes Physics

From the beginning and in principle
I am made up of balance and passion,
doctrines and the unknowable

The earth rests her transparency in fruit
Everything about the sea leaves me nostalgic
And love is sufficient canon

Someday my name will unite with my nature
My heart will have dissolved into wings
In spite of everything, don't bind me to images

I don't want to be tested like a schoolgirl
Not with words modern or post
I reject a straitjacket name

As the skies contemplate the earth,
womb of life and death, fertile and dynamic,
thus I see changes in myself
The organic currents stir me
I take awareness from them

Ties and separations squeeze me
I recognize gifts that cover faults
And watch the North Star
grow into an oceanic love
Time works in me without feeling eccentricities,
green impulses and modesty

Between beloved hands peeks a forest:
Propellers, candles,
afternoon of drizzle and tiger fangs

Pruebo el jugo puro del limón,
escucho todo el día en amarillo

Por el trazo de mi lápiz sigo mi alma

De nada hay que quisiera presumir
La redondez esponja lo sabido

Señales ordinarias: Los arrebatos sazonan el afecto
¿Por qué seguir un desierto si hay trillos verdeantes?

Las furias me han legado sus gestos
Afrodita me ha concedido su sentido perturbador
Son las Harmonías
Pero ninguna ha llegado a la paciencia.

I taste the pure juice of lemon,
listen all day long in yellow

With the line of my pencil I follow my soul

There is nothing I'd want to presume
The circle soaks up wisdom

Ordinary signs: Rages spice the affections
Why go by desert ways if there are verdant paths?

The furies have bequeathed me their gestures
Aphrodite has granted me her perturbation
They are the Harmonies
But none has arrived at patience.

Una chichigua y una estrella

Cruces naranjas, brazos o dientes,
redención o derrota,
se desplazan por la libertad del infinito

La luna ovilla lo sobrante
Tácito recado para el corazón sigiloso

Es el tiempo de cristalerías y martillos
Una pared de piedras vibra elocuencia

En la telaraña, el insecto ve un arpa

Mis expectativas aprenden de la verdura del césped

El cuerpo se transforma en alma
En su propia sombra se oculta la crisálida
Tu alba en mis miradas se delata.

A Kite and a Star

Orange crosses, arms or teeth,
redemption or rout,
floating across the freedom of the infinite

The moon winds up the excess
Unspoken message for the tight-lipped heart

It's the time of glass and hammers
A wall of stones shivers with meaning

In the spiderweb, the insect sees a harp

My hopes learn from the turf grasses

The body transforms itself into a soul
The chrysalis hides in its own shadow
Your dawn betrays itself in my gaze.

Mercado modelo

Policroma,
hechizada por la actividad de la visión,
la plaza reduce, relumbra

La pobreza es un cuerpo vítreo
La hora, unas pulidas monedas
La pasión: Un asalto de pulpa,
de calor,
de riesgo

Las nubes no existen, más que plasma solar en su memoria

El banquete servido
La esperanza, un cocodrilo sobre la mesa
La esperanza, una langosta
Un delantal. Una sierra. Una reguera de espasmódicos pétalos de horas

La esperanza,
un oráculo de verduras y víveres en remolino

La alegría,
una masa de palabras en oraciones colgando como ropa
Un pescado tieso,
un pan de agua,
un bebé mamando sudor y leche

Perfumería de yerbabuena y tijeras

Se vive ahora. En damajuana y amuletos
Los rostros se leen. Se ofrecen. Ahora mismo se viven, se ojean, se llaman
Ahora mismo, en la jaula de tiempo y espacio,
trapecistas

Mercado Modelo[6]

Polychrome,
bewitched by the activity of vision,
the plaza shrinks, flashes

Poverty is a body made of glass
The hour, some shiny coins
Passion: An assault of pulp,
heat,
risk

Clouds don't exist, more than solar plasma in your memory

The banquet served
Hope, a crocodile on the table
Hope, a lobster
An apron. A mountain range. A conduit for the spastic petals of the hours

Hope,
an oracle of swirling greens and groceries

Gaiety,
a mash of words in speeches draped like clothing
A stiff fish,
a loaf of water,
a baby suckling sweat and milk

Perfume shop of mint and scissors

People live here. In demijohns and amulets
They read faces. They offer themselves. Now they live, they eye each other,
        they call
Right now, in the cage of time and space,
trapeze artists

Un beso es el lirio envuelto en el trapo de brillar zapatos
El papel y la moneda junto al pezón

Una escaramuza entre una policía y un mercader de ámbar
Un baño con romero, una bachata, un miembro de carey
El negro eterno o la cuerda

Uñas, parpadean al turista

Los asientos encorvan. Los brazos no alcanzan el umbral
El mercado envivece
Corrompe. Ampara. Desgasta. Reproduce
Una bestia antigua merodea su lumbre incólume.

A kiss is a lily swaddled in a shoeshine rag
The paper and the coin together with the nipple

A skirmish between a policeman and an amber-seller
A bath with rosemary, bachata music, a sea-turtle's flipper
The eternal blackness or the cord

Fingernails, winking at the tourist

The chairs are bent over. The arms cannot reach the threshold
The market enlivens.
Corrupts. Gives refuge. Wears away. Reproduces
An ancient savage raiding its undamaged fire.

Reflejo

Si por primera vez retuviera la claridad
confortadora de mi conciencia

Si mis rodillas bucearan la intimidad del árbol

Y al correr se desprendieran
piedras con criaturas vivientes

Si pudiera decir *yo*
sorprendiendo ese universo
que hasta el fin ignoramos…

Reflection

If for the first time I could reclaim the comforting
clarity of my awareness

If my knees could explore the intimacy of the tree

And if, while running, I loosened stones
containing living creatures

If I could say "I"
taking by surprise that universe
that we ignore until the end...

Taínos

El aura magnética de la montaña sobre el lago se levanta. Y en torno a ella, el oráculo de los vencidos

Conduce a rozar la ronda de sus cuerpos circulantes. Nombres de numinosas cadencias por el aire dispuestos. Flota aquí la ceniza de sus lenguas. Y casi puedo figurar, decaídas, las manos que despreciaron el oro, sacando dioses de las frutas y corazones de cristales de roca

Piso el tiempo de sus pies. Al momento se dispersan como nubes o se cierran en asedio de fuego

Extraña y breve, música nunca escrita, su auguriosa palabra procura resonancia

La iguana y el caimán mastican tiempo. La susurran. La tierra, hermética, relampaguea tinta. El horizonte, un arcano de agua y aire legibles

Sus vidas pasan, una y otra vez, por la puerta que despunta entre luna y sol.

Tainos[7]

The magnetic aura of the mountain above the lake rises. And around it, the oracle of the vanquished.

Walking their circles, the bodies touch lightly. Names of numinous cadences scattered in the air. The ash of their tongues floats toward me. And I can almost describe the descending hands that scorned gold, pulling gods from the fruit and crystal hearts from the stone.

I keep time with their feet. Suddenly they disperse like clouds or hide themselves in stockades of fire.

Strange and brief, music never written, their word resonates with portents.

The iguana and the caiman chew on time. They whisper to it. The hermetic earth flashes color. The horizon, a secret written in water and air.

Their lives pass, once and again, through the door separating moon and sun.

Ylonka Nacidit-Perdomo

extraño ejército de sueños

No tuve palabras. y la lluvia (quieto pájaro de agua) hizo que abrazara un viaje. un termino al sueño. a la felicidad que ocurre irracional. girando sobre tus ojos la noche. una ciudad que multiplica del silencio el rumor del mar. la orilla inagotable del ahora.

tantas veces que se pueda amar nominalmente las trenzas del aire. el primer y último beso en la piel del tigre que llega bastándose a sí mismo en el río del alba. al dorso del espejo que en principio es un pájaro dibujando de manera infausta. copa del tumulto de la noche. contrahecha en la memoria irrisoriamente breve de la ingenua gravedad que rueda con la claridad del día.

tal parece que después de hoy los días y las noches serán tránsfuga invierno. habitaciones complejas. espacios en madera. una geografía que insinúa soledad. sepultura de palabras. abandono a las horas. al ímpetu secreto. al *sin embargo* implacable del destino.

Pero hoy estoy en la llovizna gris despierta. mirando hacia *el sur* de manera insólita. con el regreso en la sonrisa buscada. llevando detrás un olor verde triste. la conjetura de una rara y sigilosa espera que toca las ramas de tu cuerpo. el adiós que lleva dentro tantas palabras que se bifurcan buenamente en dos que parecen estar en uno. como una casa enorme inadvertida desde el puerto. cediendo a la creciente corriente del mar. al asombro y aspavientos de tu boca.

y ahora: el amarillo en la ventana. la fuga interminable de un viernes de impaciencia que lee sobre el teléfono (hasta las doce) una rutina invadida de ternura para levantar sobre tu voz. tu voz deletreando la sonrisa. la inquieta aventura de transitar con la luna en confidencia un extraño ejército de sueños.

strange army of dreams

I had no words. and the rain (quiet water bird) made me embrace a journey. an end to the dream. to the happiness that occurs irrationally. the night revolving above your eyes. a city that multiplies from silence the rumor of the sea. the inexhaustible coastline of now.

so many times you can love, in name only, the air's tresses. the first and last kiss on the skin of the tiger that arrives, sufficient unto itself, in the river of the dawn. to the other side of the mirror that began as a bird, sketching in its fatal way. a goblet of the night's tumult. falsified in the laughably brief memory of the guileless gravity that rolls with the clarity of day.

so it seems that after today days and nights will be turncoat winter. complex rooms. spaces in wood. a geography that hints at solitude. burial of words. abandoned to the hours. to the secret impetus. to the implacable *however* of destiny.

But today I am awake in the gray drizzle. looking toward *the south* in an unaccustomed way. with the return in the sought-after smile. carrying behind it a sad green smell. the conjecture of a rare and discreet hope that touches the branches of your body. the good-bye that carries inside it so many words that split easily in two but seem to be one. like an enormous house never noticed from the harbor. yielding to the growing current of the sea. to the amazement and extravagance of your mouth.

and now: yellow in the window. the endless escape of a Friday of impatience that reads over the telephone (until twelve) a routine overcome by tenderness to rise above your voice. your voice spelling a smile. the restless adventure of passing with the moon, in secret, a strange army of dreams.

soledad

La soledad es una aurora esperando con reservas mis preguntas. es como el azar. una estrella de bondad. un rincón de enjutas hierbas.

cuando llego de la montaña oteando la ternura: la soledad arde en fiebre. levanta sus brazos abandonada a las aspas inmóviles de las espigas. rumorosa en un caracol. delirando por la triste tristeza con mustiedad de alga y el rostro amusgado. en los días siguientes (para no morir tal vez) devoraba arbustos de cerezas. hablaba en las quebradas del viento con ojos de ternura. y en los escombros de un viejo olmo rozando las sombras.

Otras veces a orillas de la noche (haciendo pausa pensativa) vuelve a la idealidad. a las mejores flores. a la silueta alargada del sol. a las copas de los montes. a los surcos de la tierra escuálida. al aire con lumbre realidad.

cuando extraño tu regreso estoy como la soledad. rondando las quebradas del río. inmóvil en la inmovilidad de la conciencia. anhelante en el solitario paisaje de la angustia. y entonces espero suplicante los signos de la lluvia. fuera de aquel círculo vacío.

solitude

Solitude is a dawn awaiting my questions with reservations. it's like chance. a star of kindness. a patch of withered grass.

when I come from the mountain peering into tenderness: solitude burns with fever. raises its arms abandoned to the motionless vanes of the seedheads. rumbling in a snail shell. raving about sad sadness with seaweed's mustiness and a mossy face. in the days that followed (so as not to die, perhaps) it devoured bushes full of cherries. spoke during breaks in the wind with tender eyes. and in the rubble of an old elm tree grazing on the shadows.

Other times on the shores of the night (pausing thoughtfully) it returns to the ideal. to the best flowers. to the lengthened silhouette of the sun. to the treetops of the mountains. to the furrows of the squalid earth. to the air with blazing reality.

when I long for your return I am like solitude. patrolling the river gorges. motionless in the immobility of awareness. yearning in the solitary landscape of anguish. and then I await like a supplicant the signs of rain. out of that empty circle.

amor. amor flotante. amor desnudo

Sobre una columna del parque respiro tu respiración profunda. arquetipos de veinte años que rasgan velozmente la redondez que asume la luna. las rendijas del pasillo en la oscuridad. un poco el jardín ahora cuando respiro repleta de dudas en la madrugada descalza. espaciada. renaciente. seguida en la mirada por estruendos sigilosos.

estoy de vuelta en las hordas de la noche. llenando páginas de mi tacto. caminando sola hacia la puerta que murmura (sin verte) una esquina apresurada en la garganta. en la oleada del oleaje de mi amor. en la camisa con lentitud de enfado y caricias.

es tu cuerpo agua tibia. escarlata y violeta al ritmo de mis manos. hasta vencer sobre tu pecho desnudo.

sé que tiemblas y me obligas a abrazarte corriendo a la redonda. sin calma ni soledad. sólo pendiente a tu prisión. al deseo que alivia mi flojedaz. la caricia que llama al movimiento de mis manos. al aire húmedo techado de tu olor. del conocimiento de las torres de tu cuerpo en arbustos. florecientes de luz.

huelo a tu difusa piel. a tus dedos en paredes de tierra suelta y rojiza. huelo a este herbario de sonrisas dulces. de hipnótica belleza. y me sorprendo de amar absortamente tus manos extendidas en torno a un espacio que avanza hacia el silencio que pide volver entre mis piernas aunando en su retirada continua un exhausto aliento de quietud. de febril paseo como nogal despierto en la espalda inmóvil del placer.

Amanece. y desde un principio sólo el café confirma mi empeño de hablar a solas. se recuesta el día como flor. caen las cuartillas anotadas que pueden hablar a lo largo de lo que pienso.

hago resúmenes de silencio. desde hace horas converso con el murmullo leve del tiempo en el círculo de luz.

love. floating love. naked love

On a column in the park I breathe your deep breathing. archetypes of twenty years that swiftly tear away the roundness taken on by the moon. the cracks in the passageway in the darkness. for a while the garden now as I breathe full of doubts in the barefoot time before daybreak. distanced. reborn. followed by the gaze of a discreet uproar.

I have come back in the hordes of the night. filling pages with my touch. walking alone toward the door that murmurs (without seeing you) a hastening corner in my throat. in the swell of the surf of my love. in the shirt with slowness of anger and caresses.

your body is warm water. scarlet and violet to the rhythm of my hands. unto victory over your naked breast.

I know you tremble and force me to embrace you running in circles. with neither calm nor solitude. only attentive to your capture. to the desire that soothes my slackness. the caress that calls to the movement of my hands. to the humid air roofed with your smell. of the knowledge of the towers of your body in the bushes. blossomings of light.

I smell of your diffuse skin. of your fingers in loose, ruddy walls of earth. I smell of this herb garden of sweet smiles. of hypnotic beauty. and I am surprised by my absorbing love of your hands extended around a space that moves toward the silence that asks to come back between my legs joining an exhausted breath of stillness in its continuous retreat. of a feverish walk like a walnut tree awake on the motionless back of pleasure.

Daybreak. and from the start only the coffee confirms my compulsion to talk to myself. the day lies down like a flower. the pages fall, annotated pages of a manuscript that can speak at length of what I think.

I summarize silence. for many hours I have been conversing with the whisper of time in the circle of light.

allí vuelvo a dormir en el círculo íntimo de mis rodillas. qué voluntaria voluntad tengo de asomarme a los avisos de ternura. a tu mirada labrada como corola de azul cielo.

estoy urgente de verte. de respirar paquetes de cigarros en tu carro. de anunciar (curiosamente) que alcanzo por tu mirada el mar. el mar de tus ojos que fluye como un estanque de peces.

Estoy a prisa. intermitente. perturbada por areniscas ventanas de los musgos. por el rostro que miro en retirada con un portafolio de humedad y olor a pino.

me he colocado en las repisas de la noche. en los nudillos de los árboles truncos. y un conglomerado de besos recuerda la lejanía. la espera. el reloj en la víspera del sueño.

amor. amor flotante. amor desnudo. enorme de levedad. ondeando en silbidos de la noche junto al estío como pájaro bullicioso que se levanta hacia el cielo.

amor. amor flotante. ocurre de verde rosa. ondulante. con una bandada de besos. alegre. llegado al infinito. sumergida en la costumbre divina de estremecimiento.

I return there to sleep in the intimate circle of my knees. what willing consent do I give to letting myself see the signs of tenderness. your furrowed glance like a sky blue halo.

I need urgently to see you. to breathe boxes of cigars in your car. to announce (curiously) that I grasp the sea through your glance. the sea of your eyes that flows like a pool full of fishes.

I am in a hurry. intermittent. unsettled by the sandstone windows of the moss. by the face I look at retreating with a portfolio of dampness and the smell of pine.

I have placed myself on the shelves of the night. in the knots of the cut-off trees. and an accumulation of kisses remembers the distance. the waiting. the clock, the evening before the dream.

love. floating love. naked love. hugeness of lightness. rippling in whistlings of the night alongside summer like a restless bird rising toward the sky.

love. floating love. instance of green rose. undulating. with a flock of kisses. happy. arriving at the infinite. overwhelmed by the divine custom of trembling.

ahora que quiero

En seis minutos este instante con la perplejidad de un árbol alrededor del tiempo. como una montaña adentro del río abierto.

(estoy tocando el aire rojo del aire) sólo el viento se ha alzado con el frágil barco que respira luz en el rumor del mar. el silencio que siento en la mirada de usted. ondeando la multitud. vendaval de peces despiertos en los ángulos del paisaje de tu rostro.

tal es el paisaje de tu rostro: infinito asombro. vuelo fugaz. curiosidad en los paralelos del lenguaje (ahora que quiero: las iniciales de tu nombre. incendiada en la ternura. en la ciudad que avanza hacia la noche agobiada por la calma de la hierba desnuda.)

now that I want

In six minutes this instant with the perplexity of a tree surrounded by time. like a mountain within the open river.

(I am touching the red air of the air) only the wind has lifted itself like the fragile boat that breathes light in the rumor of the sea. the silence I feel in the look of you. rippling the multitude. the gale of fish awake in the angles of the landscape of your face.

such is the landscape of your face: infinite amazement. fugitive flight. curiosity in the parallels of language (now that I want: the initials of your name. ignited in tenderness. in the city that advances toward night burdened by the calm of the naked grass.)

la noche está entristecida. triste de tristeza pálida

(La noche está entristecida. triste de tristeza pálida que traen las postales del fondo del mar.)

conmigo va una tormenta de sorpresa. raudales inmensos en los bordes de tu boca. una alta sonrisa girando hacia afuera. a ritmo lento entre las olas donde navegan las barcas. el aura evanescente tendida en la nostalgia. en la oscilación que llega con la oculta claridad.

inmóvil es mi desplazamiento en el sitio de mi lecho. desgajada. ardua en el agotamiento. en el clamor de despertar náufraga. tocando el vértice inesperado. la espesura frágil y fugitiva del vuelo azul (azul en el éxtasis del instante) el roce de los muros. el ahora sin pausa. sin huidas.

He tendido mis brazos a la esquina que espera un vaso transparente de la lluvia. huyo ahora que el rojo húmedo del mar (lentísimamente) es un rostro en soledad. soledad de montañas. soledad de vaivén. circulos desvaídos. acaso una aldea asomada en diciembre al olor de medusas que ondean ancladas.

el cielo es una sombra que deja tras sí un ángulo vacío. sonrosadas orillas. tersas enredaderas en tierra caliza. ondulantes líneas en una flor dulce abierta que coloca el color vino a la ausencia. ausencia que escribe nostalgias como pájaro tocando las nubes. suave. fuertemente acariciando tu sexo. itinerarios alados a la redonda como pez desnudo. desnudo por distintas humedades. por la ida y vuelta de las espigas arando *el antes* que avanza. que tropieza. despuntando la oscuridad a todo lo largo del ancho espacio donde se extiende la inmovilidad. uniforme. intensa. estacionada en la imagen de tu rostro que toca márgenes del blanco. letras de la llanura espesa extendida como viñeta en la demarcación misma del río.

(Sólo el río es un viaducto de belleza sensible al tacto. sensible al territorio de tu voz. a corolas reunidas en veintitrés segundos del girasol.)

the night is saddened. sad with pale sadness

(The night is saddened. sad with pale sadness brought by postcards from the bottom of the sea.)

with me goes a storm of surprise. immense floods along the borders of your mouth. a tall smile spinning outward. in slow rhythm among the waves where the boats sail. the evanescent aura draped in nostalgia. in the fluctuation that arrives with the hidden clarity.

my displacement is motionless on the site of my bed. torn. arduous in exhaustion. in the alarm of awakening shipwrecked. touching the unexpected peak. the fragile and fugitive thickness of blue flight (blue in the ecstasy of the instant) the touch of the walls. the ceaseless now. inescapable.

I have stretched my arms to the corner that awaits a transparent glass of rain. I run away now that the humid redness of the sea (very slowly) is a face in solitude. solitude of mountains. solitude of back and forth. dull circles. perhaps a village peeking out in December at the smell of waving anchored medusas.

the sky is a shadow that leaves behind an empty angle. blushing shores. glossy vines in chalky earth. undulating lines in a sweet open flower that sends the color of wine away. absence that writes nostalgias like a bird touching clouds. soft. strongly stroking your sex. itineraries winged all around like a naked fish. naked in different moistures. through the leaving and returning of the spikes plowing *the before* that advances. that stumbles. blunting the darkness all along the wide space where immobility stretches out. uniform. intense. stationed in the image of your face that touches the margins of whiteness. letters of the dense plain spread like a vignette along the line of the river.

(Only the river is a conduit of beauty sensitive to touch. sensitive to the territory of your voice. to corollas meeting within twenty-three seconds of the sunflower.)

la noche es un tálamo de amarillo secreto

La noche es un tálamo de amarillo secreto. disensión de costumbre. leve oscilación. tregua de sed rabiosa (a lo ancho del mar parece dormir hablando en la blancura suavizante de la luna.)

ella ha traído de mí un sonido que rompe en el viento deshabitadamente lámparas de un amarillo en teja gris. movimientos en las rendijas de un alto parque mirando la curiosidad impasible de la ventana en el agua.

la noche es una huida en la vigilia. un acuario de rasgadura celeste. un bosque despierto sobre la eternidad del tiempo. invención de mí. invención de tí. papeles en los bolsillos. alguna esperanza de ir hacia el amor.

Es la noche un náufrago total. fijar las visiones. solitario pensamiento. neutralidad que atrae. cornisas en la aspereza de las piedras. juntos: necesidad de correr en la avenida. de tocar dos mundos contiguos. un barco habitualmente distraído por el alfabeto del jardín.

es extraño viajar solo hacia la noche. afirmarse en su perenne agonía. que es agonía de placer.

the night is a wedding bed of secret yellow

The night is a wedding bed of secret yellow. customary dissension. slight fluctuation. truce of furious thirst (across the sea it seems to sleep, talking in the soothing whiteness of the moon.)

she has brought out of me a sound that vacantly breaks in the wind yellow lights in a gray tree. movements in the cracks of a high park looking at the impassible curiosity of the window in the water.

the night is an escape while standing watch. an aquarium of heavenly rending. a forest awake above the eternity of time. invention of myself. invention of yourself. papers in my pockets. some hope of going toward love.

The night is a total castaway. to pin down the visions. solitary thoughts. neutrality that attracts. cornices in the harshness of the stones. together: the need to run in the avenue. to touch two contiguous worlds. a boat habitually distracted by the alphabet of the garden.

it's strange to travel alone toward the night. to be affirmed in its perennial agony. that is agony of pleasure.

su mirada me arrojó al mundo

yo he estado envuelta en mi realidad presente. en absoluta soberanía como mujer adulta. en relación a un sujeto que se mueve. a una primera persona.

su mirada me arrojó al mundo. y la poesía fue entonces eternidad. murciélago de la noche con súbitos objetos cuando las flores dormidas en apariencia saltan sobre la esfera. sobre la nueva esfera que en torno a sí misma es relámpago. sombra de arena.

your glance launched me at the world [8]

I have been wrapped in my everyday reality. in absolute sovereignty as an adult woman. in relation to a subject who can move. to a first person.

your glance launched me into the world. and poetry was then eternity. night-flying bat with sudden objects when the flowers, seemingly asleep, leap above the globe. above the new globe that flashes like lightning as it transforms itself. shadow of sand.

hacia el sur

el mar. eterno manuscrito. regresa durmiendo con el rostro hacia el sol. bebe de la tarde las horas cuando la vida rueda un viernes en el color del tiempo.

el *sur* es un pájaro descansado en la quietud perfecta. un alfabeto de miradas. símbolos color a rosa. deleitante pausa que gira del sueño. conjuntos infinitos de reencuentro. siglos de realidad intuitiva. rumor en la lentitud del cielo. verbos. sustantivos. lenguaje de amor.

ocurre que *hacia el sur* el mar es una ciudad navegable de regreso a la lluvia. silencios en el asombro. rumor del día en las barcas que envejecen las ventanas del viento.

going south

the sea. eternal manuscript. goes back to sleep with its face toward the sun. drinks from the afternoon those hours when life rolls up a Friday in the color of time.

the *south* is a bird resting in perfect stillness. an alphabet of gazes. rosy symbols. delectable pause that spins out of the dream. infinite unions of reunion. centuries of intuitive reality. murmurs in the sluggishness of the sky. verbs. nouns. language of love.

it happens that *going south* the sea is a city navigable by returning to the rain. amazed silences. rumor of the day in boats that age the windows of the wind.

me gustan las palabras

[cuando le conocí nunca pensé que iba oír durante algún tiempo a un ser especial. extremadamente bello. lleno de multitudes y memorias que me confía].

es prodigioso haber coincidido un día de otoño donde me sentía lejana. cuando solo tenía recuerdos.

ahora que he llegado a la ventana de su vida me parece haberle conocido de antes en un lugar. tal vez. donde los ángeles a diario duermen con tristeza.

a verle. al contemplarle. percibo los paisajes de su infancia. y me hago cómplice de sus acostumbradas ilusiones. de su alfabeto mágico (ahora me hace llegar a su tiempo. a los márgenes de sus sueños. a su voz y viajes hacia adentro. a preguntas que a diario son diferentes. a ese otro lugar de la memoria involuntariamente).

su rostro me parece interminable como la acuarela en la luz.

ojos marrones. ojos café. expresan sus sensaciones, su re-encuentro o travesía prevista con la palabra a la orilla de su desnudez suelta, en los espejos que libera.

sé que vive un doblaje que lleva dentro como ejercicio repetido y conversa consigo durante las horas. para un después dócil. reversible. contrapuesto al infinito. desbordante al invierno.

yo reflexiono en los horizontes. en su profunda identidad. en sus tácticas verdades.

me gustan las palabras es mi sutil narración. es el contenido de un triángulo en trébol que asoma a mi reflexión al margen del confinamiento.

ojos castaños. ojos marrones. protagonistas de sus recuerdos. de la otredad que lleva consigo refractando nocturnamente la memoria.

words please me[9]

[when I met you I never thought I was going to hear over the course of time a special being. extremely beautiful. full of multitudes and memories that trust me.]

it's wonderful to have met one autumn day where I felt myself distant. when I had only memories.

now that I've arrived at the window of your life it seems I have met you before somewhere. perhaps. where the angels sleep with sadness every day.

seeing you, thinking about you, I perceive the landscapes of your childhood. and I am implicated in your usual illusions. in your magic alphabet (now it brings me to your time. to the edges of your dreams. to your voice and inward voyages. to questions that are different every day. to that other place of memory, unwillingly).

your face seems endless like watercolor in the light.

brown eyes. mocha eyes. express your feelings, your re-encounter or anticipated passage with the word to the shore of your easy-flowing nakedness, in the mirrors that you liberate.

I know there is a living doubleness that carries inward like repeated practice and converses with you for hours. for a meek afterward. reversible. opposed to the infinite. overflowing into winter.

I reflect on horizons. on their profound identity. on their tactical truths.

words please me is my subtle narrative. it's the triangle contained in a cloverleaf that peeks at my reflection from the margins of its confinement.

chestnut eyes. brown eyes. protagonists of your memories. of the otherness you bring with you refracting memory nightly.

todo sucede en el paisaje. en la crónica que se cierra y empieza a crecer junto al mar. cantando mientras actúo para ganar. para ganar detrás de mi yo en la intimidad con una plenitud jadeante.

everything happens in the landscape. in the page that closes and starts to grow next to the sea. singing while I act to win. to win behind my "I" in intimate contact with a gasping fullness.

antes de volver a verte había en mí una marea que permanecía abrazada al aire. representaba un vaso callado en el agua, un tiempo dentro de mí, y estaba sobre el pasado, tirando la memoria en un revés, alejada de la identidad, la identidad de una sombra. yo iba en el contingente de una ola, extrañaba un signo en el adiós. las cosas en el rumor de una rosa cerrada).

era desconcertante jugar con la poesía irreversiblemente a la quieta incertidumbre. pensaba que nada tendría sentido (merodeando en el recuerdo) la fuerza apremiante de un revés que vuelve sobre la duda y el vacío.

de vuelta a los fantasmas, el centro del porvenir es pretérito. una columna de noches en el silencio y tu rostro, pasiones. libros. viajes *hacia el sur.* la palabra irreal de la tarde indefinida en la conciencia de un instante.

cuando el instante llega (después de un triángulo a la poesía) está para maravillarse del absoluto. para hacer del trébol la pequeña interrogante. la locura o un término a orillas del ser.

allí estoy ahora, cuando los bolsillos de la ausencia despiertan una condena de ir detrás de tu espacio. de hallar un orden en las nodrizas que la eterna luz viste de escrituras místicas.

nada tan hermoso como ir detrás de tu rostro. nada tan extraño que la cristalizante sublimidad en mi conquista de amar un destino sin sentido inmediato.

y ahora qué categoría tienen mis sueños si estoy acaso en alianza con un yo de inquietud en la belleza de tu alma. y no sé si estar tristísima. paciente o defensiva.

no sé si viajar a la culpabilidad. al ahora o el nunca. no sé si, por consiguiente, hacer una ceremonia de encuentro o desencuentro. ahora cuando desacostumbro la rutina del amor y converso con las horas que se escapan.

nothing more beautiful than going behind your face

before I saw you again a tide within me remained, embraced in air. it seemed a vessel kept quiet in water, a time within me, and it was about the past, shifting memory into reverse, far from identity, the identity of a shadow. I was a portion of a wave, longing for a sign in goodbye. something in the murmur of a closed rose).

it was disturbing to play irreversibly with poetry in such quiet uncertainty. I thought that nothing would make sense (pillaging memory) the urgent force of a reversal which turns on doubt and emptiness.

turn back to phantoms, the center of the future is the past tense. a column of nights in the silence and your face, passions. books. journeys *southward*. the unreal word of the indefinite afternoon in the awareness of an instant.

when the instant comes (after a triangle to poetry) it is here in order to marvel at the absolute. to make of the cloverleaf a little questioner. madness or a limit to the borders of being.

I am there now, when the pockets of absence awaken a penalty for going beyond your space. to find order in the nurturers that the eternal light dresses in mystical writings.

nothing as beautiful as going behind your face. nothing as strange as the crystallizing sublimity in my conquest of loving a destiny without immediate sense.

and now in what category do my dreams belong if I sometimes am allied with an I of uneasiness within the beauty of your soul. and I don't know whether to be very sad. patient or defensive.

I don't know whether to journey toward guilt. toward the now or the never. so I don't know whether to make a ceremony of meeting or of not meeting. now when I am out of the routine of love and converse with the escaping hours.

sin embargo, estoy aquí con mis palabras, con un portafolio que se cierra, ante un evento fortuito, sin elección.

[no obstante: es maravilloso re-encontrarte, sentir el asombro de tus ojos, y la deslumbrante sonrisa de tu rostro].

ya que el tiempo se viste de amarillo (en el paisaje de un armario que queda cerrado) me levanto para organizar mi mirada. observo sólo tu rostro. la lluvia de algo. algo que muchas veces busqué.

however, I am here with my words, with a portfolio that closes, before a fortuitous event, without choice.

[nevertheless: it is marvelous to see you again, to feel the amazement of your eyes, and the blinding smile of your face.]

since time dresses in yellow (in the landscape of a closed wardrobe) I get up to organize my gaze. I observe only your face. the rain of something. something I have often searched for.

espacio verde el paisaje, la soledad vuela en una flauta

[el aire sostiene inmóvil la mirada que el viento pinta perenne y solitariamente. si no fuera real el amor por las ventanas no retornaría el recuerdo. la ciudad moriría sin huésped. y la nada apoyada en los duendes despertaría en una alfombra empujada al sueño vestida con viejos vestidos y una multitud de escombros].

todo llueve. las murallas están en los oídos. en el territorio de raptos que escapan como aves. ingenuas y sucesivamente. como flores en las barcas de los lirios.

[cada día en la ciudad las olas se marchan en una página que va *hacia el sur*. viajan. olvidan escaleras. el absurdo en los bolsillos. un triángulo donde se leen detalles de tu rostro. el eterno ruido de las piedras. el bosque que guarda el tiempo y columnas de espejo].

green space the landscape, solitude flies in a flute

[air holds the glance motionless that the wind paints perennial and all alone. but if love were not real, memory would not return through the windows. the city would die without a guest. and the nothingness resting on the *duendes* that would wake on a carpet pushed to sleep dressed in old clothes and tatters.]

everything rains. the walls are in the ears. in the territory of abductions that escape like birds. candid and successively. like flowers in the lily boats.

[every day in the city waves march across a page which is *going south*. they travel. they forget stairways. absurdity in pockets. a triangle where details of your face can be read. the eternal racket of stones. the woodland that keeps watch over time and mirrored columns.]

la mirada despierta la afirmación apenas perdida

la mirada despierta la afirmación a veces perdida. a veces los recuerdos. a veces momentos que vencen el miedo. todas las tristezas. la lluvia. el estremecimiento de ir ausente a contemplar las estrellas. la custodia de las olas. el náufrago de ser fábula. horizonte. tormenta.

en la marcha hacia la noche la luna lleva blancas señales. polvorientas calles del pavimento descalzo. criaturas en la crecida del río. entristecida soledad. lámparas. libros. el viento húmedo. sombras sofocadas. pétalos en la irrealidad de la mirada.

the glance awakens the affirmation hardly lost

the glance awakens the affirmation sometimes lost. sometimes memories. sometimes moments which triumph over fear. all the sadnesses. rain. the trembling of going missing to contemplate the stars. the custody of the waves. the shipwreck of being fabled. horizon. storm.

moving toward night the moon carries white tokens. dusty streets of barefoot pavement. creatures in the swollen river. saddened solitude. lamps. books. the damp wind. suffocating shadows. petals in the unreality of the glance.

sólo tu rostro, amor, es un caracol de orquídea

sólo tu rostro, amor, es una larga antología de sueños. aves que escapan ingenuas. multitud de escombros al subir el día plural en la escalera, triángulo que llueve todo, la ciudad, las olas encontradas, la mirada que guarda la tarde.

[llueve. y el paisaje es un espacio verde. palabras olfativas de oquedad. y en los remos de mis manos el agua empuja viejos puentes y algas.

sólo tu rostro, amor, es el recuerdo. inmóvil cielo. ver el mar por la ventana de olor arena y frío intenso.

sólo tu rostro, amor, es un caracol de orquídea. y a ratos frágil [llorando en los nudos de tu boca] montañas de palabras].

only your face, love, is a seashell of orchids

only your face, love, is a long anthology of dreams. birds that escape, ingenuous. piles of rubbish as the manifold day climbs the stairs, triangle that rains on everything, the city, the encountered waves, the look that saves the afternoon.

[it's raining. and the landscape is a green space. words that can be sniffed out in the hollows. and with the oars of my hands, water pushes old bridges and seaweeds.

only your face, love, is the memory. unmoving heaven. to see the ocean through the window of sand smell and bitter cold.

only your face, love, is a seashell of orchids. and sometimes fragile [weeping in the knots of your mouth] mountains of words.]

su nombre

[cierto es, ya existía. le contemplaba en un oleaje de pájaros, en inmóviles brisas. estaba reclamándome que le abrazara, que le abrazara junto al aire, justo de tarde, cuando los ruidos son evidentes y las mangas de mi camisa en la línea de la luz son una reja, o a fin de cuentas, un momento que viene del recuerdo, nada que atañe al olvido, porque ahora no quedan excusas; está aquí, breve, con el rostro de la luna, con sus ojos sobre las calles, con dudas de cantos, con datos sobre el amor, desdibujando las hojas secas, que es sólo sonrisa, secretos y espera].

enero—su nombre es un espejo extendido. multitud rocosa. proximidad a la entrada de ese espacio que imagina. que ha llamado incluso sin orden alguna. su nombre es alguien que aguarda *ver* el mundo en su totalidad alrededor del día que el frío llena de azul en el horizonte para inventar el amor. las palabras. las viejas luces que el bosque hace oscuras.

su voz es el sonido de su nombre lleno de ríos. de ecos que giran. que buscan la complejidad del *sur*. el paisaje. la arena. los verbos.

sé que le hice descansar, y me alejaba triste a mirarle, imperturbable, para llegar a su identidad residente en murmuraciones en blanco.

[sus ojos están fijos, techando palabras desde una ventana donde la noche se apoya y sonríe a los árboles, desde un permanente círculo para tocar el agua, el aire fresco, los rótulos del tedio, un náufrago que significa hechicera simpatía ¿aquello que recuerda con nostalgia?, extendiendo las manos para oír, para oír lo que llega al final del invierno y la lluvia que fija el polvo.

bien pudiera atraparle, sólo para vivir el juego, las inmensas llamas que queman por el azar o el vientre del agua].

mayo—son tantas contingencias que pienso amarle como es, antítesis entre su yo y su reemplazo, dócil, con encantos, aún estando a salvo en la multiplicidad de sus intensidades.

your name[10]

[it still existed, certainly. I contemplated it in a sea-surge of birds, in motionless breezes. I was calling it to myself in order to embrace you, to couple you to the air, up against the afternoon, when sounds are clear and the sleeves of my shirt outlined in light are like latticework, or when all is said and done: a moment that comes from memory, nothing pertaining to forgetting, because now we have no excuses left; it's here, concise, with the countenance of the moon, with your eyes above the streets, with the doubts of songs, with facts on love, blurring the dry leaves, what is only a smile, secrets and waiting.]

January—your name is a mirror stretched out. rocky multitude. nearness to the door of this imaginary space. what has called out to something even without order. your name is someone who waits to *see* the world in its totality around the day that the cold fills with blue to the horizon in order to invent love. the words. the old lights that the forest darkens.

your voice is the sound of your name filled with rivers. of turning echoes. that search for the complexity of *south*. the landscape. the sand. the verbs.

I know that I made you rest, and it left me sad to see you, imperturbable, to arrive at your resident identity in blank gossipings.

[your eyes are fixed, words forming roofs beyond a window where the night leans and smiles at the trees. beyond a permanent circle to touch the water, the air fresh, the billboards of boredom, a shipwreck that signifies sympathetic magic—what to remember with nostalgia?—reaching the hands out in order to hear, to hear what comes at the end of winter and the rain that settles the dust.

it would be good to catch you, just to live the game, the immense flames that burn by accident or the belly of the water.]

May—there are enough possibilities that I think I love you like this, antithesis between your I and your replacement, docile, enchanting, even being safe from the multiplicity of your intensities.

su nombre es un interludio de nostalgia, nostalgia enfermiza, nostalgia de asombro, nostalgia de amor, un contra-símbolo, temperamento y discernimiento.

su nombre está lleno de hechizos. ha caminado largamente, ostensible, perturbando sueños, ese viaje presente que vigila, con la sensación que vuelve entre las olas del río abierto y hablar noctámbulo.

su nombre es una bahía. reminiscencias. recuerdo de un viaje para hablar de su destino y el mío con emociones ardientes y variadas, con la vehemencia que es muy cercana a la intensidad de la poesía.

su nombre es un mar-rumoroso. incesante rumor. incesante decir. calma en el silencio para huir como siempre de sí.

octubre—sigo buscándole tristemente en la plaza, donde se posan las aves, para tocar, para dar vueltas o rodar sobre una rueda que va hacia arriba y gira en forma de eclipse para gritarle que venga.

[...siempre...siempre es un círculo de lánguidos meses, crecientes, ocupados por la distancia que la ilusión llena de palabras comunes, de fríos que transporta los sauces y la sombra desde la eternidad...].

no obstante, camino por los círculos que comenta la ternura revisando su equipaje, sus códigos secretos, esa nueva y hermosa lectura del presente que los viernes adornan de alegría, de mareas que fluyen y refluyen a la derecha del paisaje en las montañas del paralelo de las aguas, del movimiento que demora al viento en sus escondrijos.

noviembre—su nombre es sólo un juego, quiere hacer que vayamos muy cerca, de brazos y manos, para pensar en su *soledad final, ya que sólo existe por mi poesía* con la visión de *un pez en piscis*].

diciembre—vendrá siempre durante las mañanas. fatigará los círculos, las veinticuatro horas del día, como un río azul en el mar. en la puesta y salida del sol. con una voz distante en la tristeza].

your name is an interlude of nostalgia, sickening nostalgia, nostalgia of awe, nostalgia of love, a countersign, temperament and discernment.

your name is full of bewitchment. it has traveled for a long time, visible, disturbing dreams, this present journey that keeps watch, with the sensation that comes between the waves of the open river and sleepwalking speech.

your name is a bay. reminiscences. record of a journey to talk about your destiny and mine with ardent and diverse emotions, with a vehemence very close to the intensity of poetry.

your name is a rumbling ocean. incessant rumbling. incessant speech. calm in the silence to flee, as always, from itself.

October—I keep searching for you sadly in the plaza, where the birds gather, to touch, to walk to and fro or roll upon a wheel that rises and turns like an eclipse to shout to you that I'm coming.

[...always...always it's a circle of languid months, growing, busy with the distance that illusion fills with ordinary words, coldness that the willows and the shadow carry beyond eternity....]

in any case, I walk along the circles that expound on tenderness reviewing your baggage, your secret codes, today's new and beautiful lecture that Fridays adorn with happiness, of tides that flow and flow again to the right of the landscape in mountains that run parallel to the waters, of the movement that holds back the wind in its hiding places.

November—your name is only a game, you want to bring us close together, in arms and hands, in order to think in your *final solitude, what only exists for my poetry* with the vision of *a fish in Pisces.*]

December—you will always come in the morning. you will be tired of circles, the twenty-four hours of the day, like a blue river in the sea. in the position and departure of the sun. with a voice distant in sadness.]

mayo—ahora tú recorres la ciudad con rótulos de cosas sin sentido, con tu cálida y hermosa sonrisa, con tu rostro de asombro, con palabras literalmente divertidas y extensas; tal vez, quizás, posiblemente, de espaldas a los laberintos, a la mirada o el cristal donde la soledad se cumple por sí, en sí y hasta de sí.

[esa es su trampa, su trampa valiente, a la cual ha dado vueltas para mirar la rueda y fábula de su destino].

marzo 10—cierto es, eres la poesía-en-el-poema, el ritmo del color de la palabra. yo sé que sientes terminar este irrevocable invierno. sé que estás allí, y pienso si recordarte o dejarte en tu sola soledad.

May—now you cross the city with the signboards of unfeeling things, with your warm and beautiful smile, with your countenance of amazement, with words literally diverting and spacious; sometimes, maybe, possibly, backward into the labyrinths, into the glance or the crystal where solitude acts on its own behalf, in itself and unto itself.

[this is your snare, a valiant snare, the way I keep going back to watch the wheel and fable of your destiny.]

March 10—it is certain that you are the poetry in the poem, the rhythm of the color of the word. I know that you sense the ending of this irrevocable winter. I know that you are there, and I think about whether to remember you or leave you in your lonely loneliness.

Notes on the Poems

Aída Cartagena Portalatín was noted, among other things, for her experiments with typography. To the extent possible, both the English and the Spanish versions in this volume retain the typographical details visible in her *Obra poética completa (1944–1984)*, the complete works published in 2000 by the Colección de la Biblioteca Nacional, Santo Domingo, Dominican Republic.

[1] "Elegy for Elegies": Moca is a Dominican city.

[2] "Elegy for Elegies": "Lilís" was the nickname of 19th-century Dominican dictator Ulises Heureux.

[3] "Elegy for Elegies": Juan Pablo Duarte was the founding father of Dominican independence (1844).

[4] "black memories": In Spanish news reports, Sharpeville, South Africa, often appears as Shaperville.

[5] "The Landscape's Deathly Pallor": Francisco Gómez de Quevedo y Villegas (1580–1645) was one of the leading poets and satirists of Spain's Golden Age. His works ranged from the obscene to the devout. He is perhaps best remembered for his picaresque novel *La vida del buscón* (*The Life of a Scoundrel*) (1626).

[6] "Mercado Modelo": an indoor market in Santo Domingo. In addition to handicrafts and souvenirs, it is known for *botánicas* selling herbs, spices, amulets and potions.

[7] "Tainos": The Tainos were the indigenous people of Hispaniola, enslaved by the Spanish and considered extinct by the early 17th century.

[8] "your glance launched me at the world": In this poem and two that follow, Ylonka Nacidit-Perdomo uses the object pronoun "le" and the possessive pronoun "su." These pronouns are ambiguous—"le" can refer to "him," "her" or "you," formal (and hence not intimate); "su" can refer to "his," "her" or "your," formal and even plural. Because the ambiguity is intended by the author, the translator has chosen "you," recognizing that the ambiguities available to the original poet cannot be rendered in English.

[9] "words please me": see note 8.

[10] "your name": see note 8.

Acknowledgments

The translator thanks the editors of the following print and online journals, where some of the translations of poems by Ylonka Nacidit-Perdomo first appeared:

The Bitter Oleander: "solitude," "now that I want," and "the night is a wedding bed of secret yellow";

The Refined Savage: "the night is a wedding bed of secret yellow," "now that I want," and "love. floating love. naked love."

The Spanish-language poems in this collection were originally published as follows:

Aída Cartagena Portalatín: *Obra poética completa (1944-1984)*. Santo Domingo: Colección de la Biblioteca Nacional, 2000.

Ángela Hernández Núñez: *Arca Espejada*. Santo Domingo: Editora Buho, 1994; *Telar de Rebeldía*. Santo Domingo: Colección Espacios Culturales, 1998. *Alicornio*. Santo Domingo: Editorial Cole, 2004.

Ylonka Nacidit-Perdomo: *Papeles de la Noche*. Santo Domingo: CLDEH (Crítica Literaria Dominicana Sobre Escritoras Hispanoamericanas), 1998; *Hacia el Sur*. Montreal and Santo Domingo: CCLEH (Crítica Canadiense Literaria Sobre Escritoras Hispanoamericanas), 2001.

The translator wishes to thank the Fulbright Program of the United States Department of State and Saginaw Valley State University for support of her research in the Dominican Republic during the winter and spring of 2002. Dr. Gustavo Batista, Rector of UNIBE (Universidad Iberoamericana) in Santo Domingo, generously allowed me time and facilities to work. Without their support, the work on this book would not have been possible.

¡Mil gracias! to Linda M. Rodríguez Guglielmoni, who provided the lion's share of the introduction as well as consultation on the translations and proofreading, and to the University of Puerto Rico–Mayagüez for providing her with time to work on this project.

Thanks also to Ann Garcia, my language consultant, for her invaluable contributions on the details of the translations.

About the Authors

Aída Cartagena Portalatín (1918–1994) was one of the most significant 20th-century woman authors of the Dominican Republic. Poet, fiction writer, historian, art critic, university professor, and mentor to younger writers, she published eight poetry collections, two novels, and a short story collection, as well as important ethnographic papers on African and Amerindian elements in Dominican culture.

Ángela Hernández Núñez (b. 1954) studied Chemical Engineering and taught Chemistry at Universidad Autónoma de Santo Domingo. During the 1980s she was a leader in the national feminist movement. She has published five poetry collections, five short story collections, and two novels (Cole Prize winner, 2002), as well as essays on civil rights and women's issues. She lives in Santo Domingo, D.R.

Ylonka Nacidit-Perdomo (b. 1965) studied Law and Political Science at Universidad Autónoma de Santo Domingo. Poet, essayist, and literary critic, she has been a leading editor, publisher, and promoter of literary works by Dominican women and served as Director of Research at the Dominican National Library. She has published seven poetry collections and numerous essays about Dominican literature. She lives in Santo Domingo, D.R.

About the Translator

Judith Kerman translated Dominican women's poetry and fiction as a Fulbright Senior Scholar in the Dominican Republic in 2002. She has published *A Woman in Her Garden: Selected Poems of Dulce María Loynaz* (translations, White Pine Press, 2002), eight books and chapbooks of her own poems, and numerous poems and translations in journals and anthologies.

Linda María Rodríguez Guglielmoni co-wrote the Introduction to this volume. Her Ph.D. dissertation at the University of Michigan–Ann Arbor, "Historical Narratives in the Caribbean: Women Giving Voice to History," included a chapter on Aída Cartagena Portalatín. She has published poetry, translations, and scholarly articles on Caribbean and women's literature.

The Lannan Translations Selection Series

Ljuba Merlina Bortolani, *The Siege*

Olga Orozco, *Engravings Torn from Insomnia*

GérardMartin, *The Hiddenness of the World*

Fadhil Al-Azzawi, *Miracle Maker*

Sándor Csoóri, *Before and After the Fall: New Poems*

Francisca Aguirre, *Ithaca*

Jean-Michel Maulpoix, *A Matter of Blue*

*Willow, Wine, Mirror, Moon:
Women's Poems from Tang China*

Felipe Benítez Reyes, *Probable Lives*

Ko Un, *Flowers of a Moment*

Paulo Henriques Britto, *The Clean Shirt of It*

Moikom Zeqo, *I Don't Believe in Ghosts*

Adonis (Ali Ahmad Sa'id), *Mihyar of Damascus, His Songs*

Maya Bejerano, *The Hymns of Job and Other Poems*

Novica Tadić, *Dark Things*

Praises & Offenses: Three Women Poets from the Dominican Republic

For more on the Lannan Translations Selection Series
visit our Web site:
www.boaeditions.org

❖